THE MIRACLE THAT IS

YOUR

LIFE

Wendy L. Darling, M.Ed., Sp.Ed.

The Miracle That Is Your Life

by Wendy L. Darling

All rights reserved. No part of this publication may be reproduced, distributed, or transmitted in any form or by any means, including photocopying, recording, or other electronic or mechanical methods, or by any information storage and retrieval system, without the prior written permission of the publisher and author, except in the case of brief quotations embodied in critical reviews and certain other non-commercial uses permitted by copyright law.

Copyright © 2014 by Wendy L. Darling
Cover Design by Melodye Hunter

ISBN: 978-0-9909974-4-3 (p)
ISBN: 978-0-9909974-5-0 (e)

Crescendo Publishing, LLC
300 Carlsbad Village Drive
Ste. 108A, #443
Carlsbad, California 92008-2999

A Message from the Author...

Click on the video or the link to hear a personal message from Wendy L. Darling, author of The Miracle That Is Your Life

http://youtu.be/VwfNE1uTK9g

To further support you on your journey, remember to download your free bonus gifts, available at http://wendydarling.com/book-bonuses/

*This book is dedicated
to the two men
who have meant the most to me,
who have inspired me to be a better person
and to appreciate
the life I have been given.*

*I dedicate this
book to
Nelson J. Lackritz, my father
and
Adam N. Pitchie, my son.*

*And to the third man,
Whom God and my 'two dads' have chosen for me to
Share the rest of my life
I am forever grateful,
I honor and celebrate the miracle of you.*

Table of Contents

FOREWORD   1

INTRODUCTION 7

Chapter 1: My Personal Journey 11

Chapter 2: Magic Wand Time.. 19

Chapter 3: Entry Points.. 33

Chapter 4: Michelangelo and You 47

Chapter 5: Where's the Gap 53

Chapter 6: The Positioning and Driving Forces of Your Values 63

Chapter 7: Good Vibrations – It's All About Energy! 75

Chapter 8: The Value of Your Vision 83

Chapter 9: The Magic of Your Mind................................... 93

Chapter 10: The Power of Your Heart 103

Chapter 11: Your Body Is the Temple for Your Soul ... 111

Chapter 12: Focus on MEE 117

Chapter 13: How Do We Get Off Course and Out of Alignment in the First Place? 127

Chapter 14: Bringing Harmony into Your Heart and Mind 143

Chapter 15: Mischief Makers 153

Chapter 16: Speed Bumps, Detours and Roadblocks 169

Chapter 17: Healing Harmonics™ and Your Signature Soul Song™ 179

Chapter 18: Putting Your Miracle of Life Method into Practice 185

Chapter 19: Finding H.O.M.E. 193

About the Author 201

Connect with Wendy 205

In Gratitude to You 207

FOREWORD

To My Readers,

As a five-time global and *New York Times* best-selling author myself, I can almost twinkle when a new "best seller" is about to sweep the world. I was there when record-breaking projects like *Chicken Soup for the Soul* were birthed. I was there when Men and Mars collided (for real). I was there when *Rich Dad Poor Dad* was led by lady leaders like Sharon Lechter, who went on to better Robert with *Outwitting the Devil* and *Think and Grow Rich for Women*, outperforming her prior records one after the other. I was there when Sharon and Greg launched *Three Feet from Gold*, and Bob Proctor asked us to promote *The Secret* before he even appeared in the film and Lisa Nichols' book, *No Matter What*. In fact, google "CEO SPACE Lisa Nichols" and see her film confirming all the forgoing so that you are sure I'm not fudging.

Wendy Darling is not just another author nor is her book just another publication. Wendy Darling has, for years, advanced my wife September's and my own work on the planet and in this lifetime. Her work with us spans a weekly session, one with myself and a separate, private session with my September. As a lady leader, September runs CEO SPACE in 140 nations, and as president and COO commands worldwide respect for her contribution to small businesses globally.

During our sessions, September and I may discuss issues with one another, with our own future growth, with the business—anything. Wendy can decide what to share one to the other with total open regard for our trust in her "knowing." Out of all the legendary mentors on our CEO SPACE faculty, including John Gray, Bob Proctor, Jack Canfield, Harv, Greg Reid, Les Brown, Lisa Nichols, Sharon Lechter, Barrnett Bain, Cathy Lee Crosby, David Stanley, Gene Kirkwood, Michelle Patterson, Kelly Holmes, Tony Robbins, and so many more, we cannot advance the premise of, if we choose Wendy Darling, how advanced and bleeding edge must her work truly be? If we have faithfully profited from her work products in both our personal and professional lives (and for which, we can't express enough gratitude), what must this work be like, given the publications we have named here that set new records in the market space?

The Miracle That Is Your Life dramatically appreciates that we all have only one bank account, which came into a single deposit when we were born. This bank account keeps the single deposit of our total "life time". Our single asset. Every hour the power of that one hour is lost forever and withdrawn from our "balance" in this Earth walk. We can never slow down the flow. We can never change the pace. We can never reclaim one prior hour of power.

How you will use your divine bank account is the only question to consider when discussing what comes next into your living of your own life. Hey, good and bad things happen out there. I've had $500 million closing days, and those were good days, let me tell you. I've had days of self-surrendering to a federal prison for a framework that was not even a crime—that was a bad hair day. Your attitude in life going into your own record closing or your own day at the farm is the defining aspect of how you live the MIRACLE of your OWN LIFE.

Wendy creates a process to self-audit your bank account. Where are you now in YOUR life time? Where have you been? Where are you going next? What do you want to improve? What do you wish to let go of? What do you wish to achieve? How will you use your lifetime differently after you have read this book? I've been told my book, *Redemption: The Cooperation Revolution,* is the only book since the Bible that actually reads YOU while you read the book.

I believe *The Miracle That Is Your Life* is another book that actually reads you while you are reading the book. I believe you will have a different future. A better tomorrow. A more peaceful, joyous use of the remainder of your lifetime.

The Miracle That Is Your Life is a perfect "thank you" gift for your customers. You will ensure client loyalty, repeat buying, and referral marketing. Gift my Wendy's book as you buy at least TEN and give this book to those you wish to acknowledge with gratitude. They will remember your gift for the remainder of their lifetime. Your memory to them will be sweeter and forever.

Wendy Darling has made the most dramatic shift in our marriage—already great and now FANTASTIC—in our business, and in our third-party communications. We see with new eyes. We are more grateful for our POWER HOURS, and we are more appreciative of everyone in our lives. So much more appreciative. As Dolly Parton said online recently, "My God, honey, I've got so many problems in my own life I don't have the ability or time to judge someone else on their life."

You let go of the junk files on your mind's computers.

You delete the fragments that remained behind from earlier deletions.

You purge.

You grow disk space.

You grow your RAM and your hard drive capacity.

In fact, reading the *The Miracle That Is Your Life* is a virtual upgrade for your soul while your life is unfolding.

Are you starving for more companionship in life? Starving to be heard—just really heard and understood? Are you seeking? Seeking more? Are you hungry for kindness? Needing a snack of generosity? Do you need to see a world different from the one that news salespeople try and have us buy into? Do you wish for more forgiveness and LOVE in your next POWER HOUR?

With Wendy's release of *The Miracle That Is Your Life*, you no longer have to wait. You can have a more perfect life right now. I wrote the book *Perfection Can Be Had!* and I believe Wendy has written a far better sequel.

Share this work with those you love.

That's my most important message. If you have read *Chicken Soup* or *Women are from Venus and Men are From Mars* or *Rich Dad Poor Dad* or *Outwitting the Devil* or even heard of *The Secret*, this book will belong to each of you in that same special way.

Read this work as a child.

Be heart-open like a young child.

Allow your trust in Wendy to mirror our own as her vast experience comes to benefit your life.

If you ever get the chance to see Wendy Darling LIVE, drop everything—reschedule everything—and make that moment happen. You will participate in something far more than a simple training, for you and those you share the experience beside will have shared a historical event.

Reading *The Miracle That Is Your Life* is and will forever be a historical event in your life.

I know I'm years living the principles of the book guided by Wendy Darling personally.

What a privilege to our family and community.

THANK YOU WENDY DARLING!!

Berny Dohrmann
Chairman, CEO SPACE INTERNATIONAL

INTRODUCTION

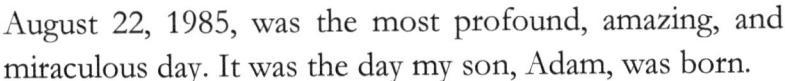

August 22, 1985, was the most profound, amazing, and miraculous day. It was the day my son, Adam, was born.

The minute I found out I was pregnant I was filled with such happiness! My husband and I had been discussing whether and when to have children. And, since we were not in full agreement, we decided to table the discussion for a couple months. Little did either of us know at the time—I was already pregnant.

I enjoyed every moment of being pregnant. Other than a little fatigue in the early days, I had never felt happier or healthier. I was fascinated with how this being was growing inside my body. I delighted when I felt his first butterfly-like movements. And as he grew, I was fascinated with the entire experience.

When I held my son in my arms for the first time, I could not stop staring at him. My mind swam with curiosity as to how a moment of fun and frolic produced this amazing person.

Six weeks later, I made arrangements to return to Cincinnati, where my mother lived, to have a baby naming for my son. In Judaism, it is tradition to give your child a Hebrew name. It is also customary to give a name in memory of those who were already deceased.

My father had passed away two years before, and I wanted to honor his life. My dad meant the world to me. He was such an amazing man, with a generous heart, and he really believed in me. He always encouraged me to follow my heart and go for my dreams. And he made me believe that anything was possible to achieve.

Yet, when he died, my world felt rather unsettled. So I now had the opportunity to keep his spirit alive within the relationship with my son.

My father's Hebrew name was Nissan. The translation means "miracle." How perfect! I truly was in awe of my little miracle boy!

In addition to my father, my husband's grandfather had also recently passed away, so I inquired what the Hebrew name for Charles was. The rabbi informed me it was Chaim, which translates to "life."

So we gave Adam his Hebrew name: Nissan Chaim. And the English translation is:

THE MIRACLE OF LIFE!

I could hardly believe my ears when the rabbi first shared this with me. The perfection of his name made my heart sing.

Adam was the greatest gift I had ever received AND he truly was and is a miracle of life!

I had always been able to see the miracles of my son's life, as well as those with whom I came in contact. However, I struggled to see my own! Isn't that interesting?

My journey has not been the easiest, and yet I have come full circle to appreciate the miracle of MY life, as well as the lives of others.

I invite you to come on this journey with me.

Together, we are going to explore the richness of who you are, the gifts you are destined to share, and the magic and miracles that life has to offer.

By the end of this book, not only do I want you to know, in every fiber of your being, that YOU are a walking miracle, but also that your life is a miracle for YOU … and for you to share.

Wendy L. Darling

Chapter 1

My Personal Journey

Wendy L. Darling

-1-

My Personal Journey

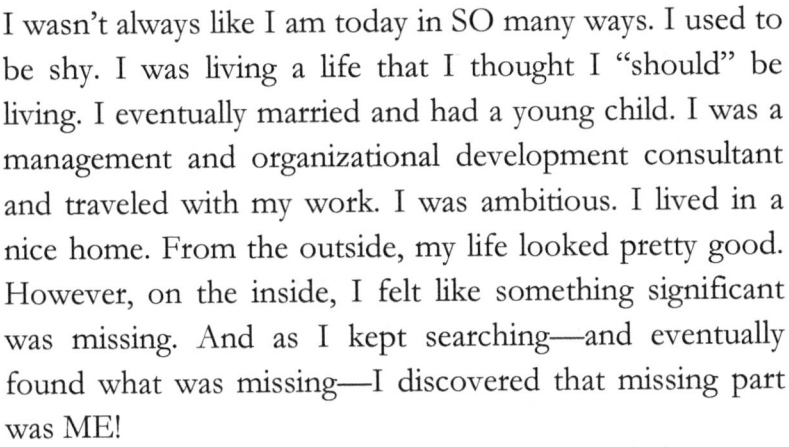

I wasn't always like I am today in SO many ways. I used to be shy. I was living a life that I thought I "should" be living. I eventually married and had a young child. I was a management and organizational development consultant and traveled with my work. I was ambitious. I lived in a nice home. From the outside, my life looked pretty good. However, on the inside, I felt like something significant was missing. And as I kept searching—and eventually found what was missing—I discovered that missing part was ME!

There was a stirring within me that, for a significant amount of time, I ignored. And finally it all came to a head.

I had been on a rather rigorous travel schedule, working with a Fortune 100 company, travelling all over the country for them. I had not been taking good care of myself. I was eating poorly. I was not sleeping much. As I prepared for another trip, I was very sick. Yet my work ethic had me determined to get on the plane and make certain I fulfilled my commitment.

Unfortunately, that never happened.

I got as far as the Dallas/Ft. Worth airport. Feeling nauseous, I went outside the airport to get some fresh air. While outside, I passed out and fell over a ledge, falling approximately twenty-five feet.

I was taken to the hospital where doctors discovered I had shattered one of my legs, and my back was broken. Initially, it was uncertain if my leg could be saved. It took more than ten months and multiple surgeries before I knew if I would ever walk again. And I was later diagnosed with a traumatic brain injury from which it took me years to recover. (Although I have never had a full recovery, I am blessed to be doing VERY well!)

My injured body, however, was only a mere reflection of how my life was broken and shattered. While in the hospital, my (then) husband came to me with my suitcases packed, saying he was no longer willing to be married to me anymore. We had been struggling with our marriage for some time, and even though I could not fault him for wanting to throw in the towel, it was still devastating, and the timing was challenging.

You see, I had made some HUGE mistakes in my choices. I liked the attention I was getting in my work, the validation of what I could offer, the changes of which I was a part. But I neglected and violated the commitments I had made to my husband. Yes, I had been unfaithful. I am being completely open and honest here because this is one of the biggest regrets I have had in my entire life, and it has been at the core of what has propelled me on my journey to discovering who I really am. I wanted to know how I possibly could have made those choices—choices that I would NEVER make again. And I also wanted to know how and in what way I had gotten so off track. I wanted to know how to find ME. I wanted to discover more about how I could contribute my gift and skills.

You see, the night before my accident, in my weakened state, I confessed to my husband that I had been unfaithful. I confessed because I could no longer live with the lie. I knew he was deeply hurt. I can only imagine what it is like to feel like you are living with someone you thought you could trust—the one person who was to be there for you, to make your world a safe and better place—and then to find out you had been so severely betrayed. That is a very deep violation and wound.

And now this hurt was directed at me. And it was payback time. And it was payback I got.

My former husband is an attorney, and the greatest blow was when we went to court and he was awarded full custody of our four-year-old son. Something inside me snapped, and it took MANY years to recover.

I kept wondering how I had managed to get into this messy state! How had I gotten so off track that my body and life were in complete shambles? How could someone like me, with all my wisdom, have messed up so significantly? And as painful as it all was, it was also the beginning of my journey to H.O.M.E.—what I refer to as "Heaven on Earth, With ME In the Middle." It was my journey to finding out who this person, Wendy Darling, really was. And that is what I want to offer you. I want there to be no misunderstanding or mistakes. I want you to understand how very special you are—right now—and that your life REALLY matters. And I want to make sure you are experiencing H.O.M.E., too. This is your opportunity to find your special place in life and make YOUR special mark.

Today I am grateful I never gave up. I'm grateful that I kept searching for ME, for the life I knew, deep in my soul, that I was created to live.

And this is why I am writing this book.

I KNOW in every fiber of my being that each and every one of us was born with a special purpose to fulfill in life. AND I know we are to live life in joy, happiness, and prosperity ... and simply have FUN while doing it all!

Yet, as I was, so many are suffering. I believe it's my job to assist in putting that to an end and to open the floodgates for the heavens to shower you with all the richness life has to offer—to fill YOU up, so that you can fulfill YOUR destiny!

I believe I've cracked the code to help show you the way! It's actually rather simple, although it's going to take a little practice on your part. But what's a little practice in exchange for having all your dreams and desires come true?

Wendy L. Darling

Chapter 2

Magic Wand Time

Wendy L. Darling

-2-

Magic Wand Time

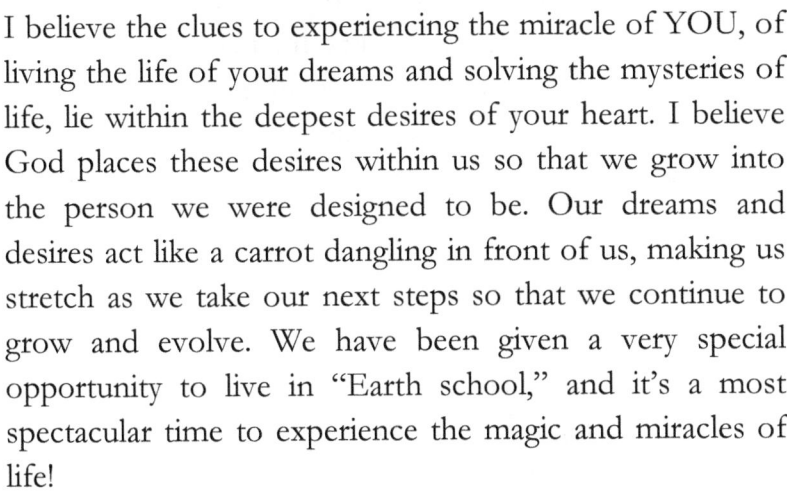

I believe the clues to experiencing the miracle of YOU, of living the life of your dreams and solving the mysteries of life, lie within the deepest desires of your heart. I believe God places these desires within us so that we grow into the person we were designed to be. Our dreams and desires act like a carrot dangling in front of us, making us stretch as we take our next steps so that we continue to grow and evolve. We have been given a very special opportunity to live in "Earth school," and it's a most spectacular time to experience the magic and miracles of life!

I also believe our deepest desires help us create the clarity to discover more about who you really are—the real you, the authentic you. And in doing so, it becomes clearer what purpose your life is to serve, the special contribution you were chosen to make. When these pieces come together, life truly becomes miraculous.

Before we go on, I would like to make a distinction between a wish and a desire. For me, a wish is simply just that: a wish. I wish I could take a trip to New York. I wish I could buy a Mercedes. I wish I would meet Mr. Wonderful.

A desire, on the other hand, holds a deeper meaning and purpose. Going to New York City may represent your business is growing and you're continuing to reach the people whom you can best serve. Or maybe it's the reward for releasing those unwanted pounds and getting your body in a healthier state. After all, having a healthy body serves you by helping you be the person you want to be. Being healthy enables you to do all the things you want to do. So what are your deepest desires?

Let's take some time to explore what you truly DESIRE. Do you know why these desires are so important to you? It's because the core part of you is reminding you that this is your TRUTH. Your dreams and desires are not within you to torture you. They are there to remind you that this is all being paved for you to experience! You have just separated yourself from knowing and receiving all the gifts God is attempting to send your way.

Isn't it time you recognize your value, your worth, and the life you were designed and destined to live?

So let's do a little exercise before going any further. I want you to imagine the life you deeply desire. Fill out the information below. Some answers may come easily to you. Other areas may be more challenging. If you experience some challenges with this, no worries. Those challenges are just showing how you have pushed your desires down so deep that you have lost hope and belief that this may be truly possible.

You may also be a person who knows COMPLETELY what your dreams and desires are, but you have not been able to realize them. However, you obviously have not given up since you have this book in your hands! GOOD!

There really is a solution, and I'm going to help you find YOUR way so that you are FINALLY living the life of your dreams! God wants that for you. AND God wants you to be able to "go for it" because God also wants you to make your special contribution! God wants you to be proud of who you are and what you have to offer, which doesn't mean that you need to be the next Oprah or Bill Gates. It means that when you walk into the room, YOU walk into the room because who you are is special, right now, just the way you are! And because you were gifted life, YOU are a walking miracle. You are the gift. And it's time to show yourself more to the world!

Recently, in one of my meditations, God said, "There is no more time to contemplate our navels! I need all my soldiers up and running." It's not only time for you to be living the life of your dreams, it's also time for you to be contributing to others, helping OTHERS experience the life of THEIR dreams, fulfilling THEIR destinies! And if you are reading this, I'm convinced you are one of those "soldiers" God was referring to.

Maybe you have a special offer. Maybe you're an amazing friend in time of need. Maybe you really are your own unique version of Oprah or Bill Gates. It's your heart that is calling out to you. It's your soul guiding you along the way. It's what makes you take a step when you don't want to. It's also the part of you that aches because you know there is so much more of life to experience, and you just haven't fully tapped into that!

So, let's have this exercise be "magic wand time"!

If you could wave your magic wand and have the life of your dreams, what would it be like?

YOUR HEALTH: What is the quality of your health? What is your optimal weight? How is your level of fitness?

_____

_____

_____

What is the deeper meaning and purpose of having optimal health? What does it provide for you? What does it allow you to experience? How does it serve your mission/purpose in life?

_____
_____
_____
_____

YOUR HOME: Where are you living? What kind of home are you living in? How is it furnished? How does it FEEL to be living in this home?

_____
_____
_____
_____

What is the meaning and purpose of having this home? How does it serve you? How might it support you in fulfilling your mission/destiny?

_____
_____
_____
_____

YOUR LOVE LIFE: Are you in a relationship? If so, what is the quality of the relationship? How are you with each other? How do you FEEL in this relationship? How do you love and contribute to this person? How do they love and contribute to you? How are you BETTER because the two of you are together?

_____
_____

_____

_____

What is the deeper meaning/purpose of having this relationship? How does having this special relationship serve you? How does it serve your mission/purpose in life? How are the gifts you receive by being together in this relationship allowing you to be a better person, to make a greater contribution?

_____

_____

_____

_____

YOUR FAMILY: What does family look like to you when you are living "heaven on Earth with me in the middle"? Who is your family? Where is your family? How are you involved with each other? What does family FEEL like to you?

_____

_____

_____

_____

What is the deeper meaning/purpose of your family? How does it serve you? How does it serve your mission/purpose in life? What are the gifts your family offers by being together? How does this allow you to be better? How might this tie into the contribution your life has to offer?

___

YOUR FRIENDS: How are the friendships in your life serving you? What kind of friend are you? Why are your friendships important and meaningful to you?

___

What might be the deeper meaning/purpose of your circle of friends? How might they be contributing to your life? How might you be contributing to theirs? How might your friendships be serving your mission/purpose in life?

___

YOUR WORK: Whether it be for pay or on a volunteer basis, what is your offer? How are you contributing to others? How are you making your mark? What brings you the greatest degree of joy and satisfaction through the work you offer?

_____
_____
_____
_____

What is the deeper purpose/meaning of your work? How is it fueling your mission/purpose? What contribution are you able to make through the work you do?

_____
_____
_____
_____

YOUR FINANCES: When it comes to your finances, what is financial "heaven on Earth with you in the middle"? What are your finances providing? How are your finances serving you? Others? What are the greatest gifts your finances are giving you?

_____
_____
_____
_____

What is the deeper meaning/purpose of your finances? What purpose does your wealth serve to you and others? How does this contribute to your ultimate desires and destiny?

_____
_____

_____

_____

YOUR COMMUNITY: How are you involved in your community? How do you contribute and support your community? What causes or organizations benefit the most from your involvement? What endeavors are you most proud of that you have been able to contribute to? Why are these causes/organizations important to you?

_____

_____

_____

What deeper meaning/purpose does your involvement in your community serve? In what ways might your involvement serve to facilitate your purpose in life?

_____

_____

_____

YOUR SPIRITUALITY: What role does your spirituality play in your life? What practices do you have in place that keep you connected to God, your soul, your guidance? How does it FEEL to take time to strengthen this connection? Why has this become important for you?

_____

_____

_____

_____

What is the deeper meaning/purpose of your spiritual practices? How does this serve a higher purpose in your life? In what way does it nourish your soul, celebrate the miracle of your life, fulfill your destiny?

_____

_____

_____

_____

FUN! What fun are you having? What kind of adventures are you creating? What does fun look like for you?

_____

_____

_____

_____

What deeper meaning/purpose is fun serving in your life? How is it nourishing your soul and fulfilling your deepest desires and destiny?

_____

_____

_____

_____

Now that you have awakened and recognized the desires of your heart, now that you know what a miraculous life looks like for you, let's begin the journey to allow that to materialize! Time to turn those dreams into reality ... NOW!!

WORDS OF ENCOURAGEMENT:

Dear God,

I thank you for giving me this wonderful opportunity called "my life." I know that life has not always been easy, but I truly believe that you have my back! I now dedicate time each day to ensure we stay connected. I know you are doing all you can to turn my dreams into reality so that, in turn, I can fulfill the destiny you created for me. Thank you for your love, your wisdom, and your support. And thank you for holding me in your arms, loving me the way you do, and gently encouraging me to blossom. I'm grateful for my life today, for all my yesterdays, and for all the tomorrows yet to come.

Chapter 3

Entry Points

Wendy L. Darling

-3-

Entry Points

In the last chapter you identified your dream life. As a reminder, this is NOT fantasy. The desires in your heart are there to help you grow and evolve into the person you were created to be. Now we just need to make sure all of that materializes!

I've always been committed to my clients getting the results they want in the easiest and fastest way possible. But many years ago, I changed the way I work with my clients. I no longer remember what had me shift and reach this conclusion, but I began to question how it might be possible to get results easier and faster.

My training in counseling psychology led me to focus on the past and healing from that perspective. Even as I became skilled in other modalities, I was still functioning from a "find it, fix it" mode. I began to question this when I realized it might actually be interfering with getting your desired results. I was always looking for what was off, wrong, and in need of healing/fixing. I began to wonder if we had been focusing in the wrong direction.

WHAT IF we focused on the desired results with a modality that could, at the same time, wash away the internal interference of the past? THAT was a novel approach at that time. Also, now that we knew more about how the mind works and the power of one's thoughts, this was beginning to make more sense.

So I decided to try an experiment on myself. I created an audio recording with this new approach and gave it a try. I had become a bit overweight, so I experimented to see if it would help me release those unwanted pounds. Not only did I release the weight, but I had physical evidence that my theory actually worked. My Healing Harmonics™ Systems was officially birthed.

It was THE EASIEST and most natural way to shift my body. And, even better, it allowed me to open up to an even more amazing life. AND, with this new approach, I was able to offer a new and improved Loving Yourself Lean, my weight-loss program I had been delivering on and off since 1991.

But soon it got even better.

Part of my system includes a unique and comprehensive diagnostic approach. I am able to easily find the root cause of what may be holding you back, even if you can't find it, even if you don't know it exists.

Then I wondered, what if I were to use an approach to help my clients determine the first steps that would allow them to get the easiest and fastest results? So I gave that a try, and I must admit I was really surprised by the way the process guided my clients to what was best for them to do. The place where a person needed to start was not always directly related to their #1 desired result, the main reason they came to work with me.

This became the birth of what I now call "Entry Points."

An entry point is just that, the starting place. It's where we focus first. It's your first step(s) that allow you to get the biggest bang for your buck. In other words, you begin with Entry Point A, and Entry Point A is the kingpin domino. When we begin there, all the other dominoes—your next steps—will fall over easily, gently, and quickly. And what is interesting, using my Healing Harmonics™ System, your Entry Point is divinely guided. My system allows you to tap into your Inner Guidance System, and it's your intuition that is navigating. It's very cool!

Let me give you an example.

One of my clients came to me because his business was losing ground—and fast. It seemed like he could not get a new client to save his soul. He was at his wits' end, and he was nearing the bottom of his finances. His wife had divorced him over a year earlier, and, to make matters worse, he wasn't feeling well and was concerned about his health.

Now, I would have rolled up my sleeves and began looking at what to do about his business and getting money flowing again.

However, in his case, his Entry Point was to begin dating!

I can assure you, I would NEVER personally recommend that. I would have wanted him to get his business up and running, get more financially stable, THEN consider dating.

But this is what I love about Entry Points. It may not make sense to you and me, but I have seen examples, time and time again, that Entry Points produce the results my clients want desperately.

So my client got online and began chatting with different women. Within a very short period of time, he met someone special. Within a shorter period of time, he began attracting clients again, and within another short period of time, he relocated to the same city and country. (YES! She lived outside the U.S.) They are together, happy, and his business is thriving.

The magic that began to happen to this man was a gift to watch. EVERYTHING he really wanted began materializing, and it all began when he focused first on his Entry Point: dating.

Of course, we also spent time on his business, but dating was his primary focus, and he scheduled times to include that into his day.

So let's examine what your Entry Point may be.

EXERCISE: Take a moment to sit quietly in a chair. Uncross your legs and sit up straight. Take a few deep breaths. While taking your breaths, identify your #1 deepest desire. Is it attracting love into your life? Creating a deeper connection with the person you are with? Creating a thriving business? Letting go of some excess weight or simply strengthening your health? Whatever it is, state that out loud.

Now, place both hands over your heart.

As you continue to breathe gently and deeply, you are going to "receive" a number 1-8. You may hear it, see it, or feel it in your heart, which then translates it for you. Take your time. This number corresponds to your Entry Point.

When you have your number, you may continue reading this chapter. (Please do not look ahead!)

To find out which category YOUR number corresponds to, go to http://wendydarling.com/book-bonuses/.

I'm going to share what each of these numbers mean. Then we are also going to explore why this may be your Entry Point.

Each of the numbers corresponds to the following categories:

Spirituality

Health

Home

Love

Family

Friends/Community

Fun

Career/Finance

Whatever your category is, this is your Entry Point. Let's take a closer look at what these Entry Points might mean for you.

Spirituality. For me, this is the foundation of how we live, the choices we make, the actions we take. If this is your Entry Point, you are being guided to take time to connect with your heart and soul. You are being guided to spend time in quiet. Maybe it's to learn how to meditate. Maybe it's simply to sit back and reflect. However, your reflection is to be time spent listening to the gentle whispers and pulls of your heart. Allow your heart to guide you. Spend time writing your thoughts, your ideas, your worries and concerns. Ask questions. Allow for answers. They may not come right away, but they will come. Give yourself time to deepen your relationship with God. Give yourself time to deepen your relationship with your heart, your feelings, your desires. Allow yourself to feel all that you are, all you are becoming.

Health. You are being guided to take better care of your health. Does this resonate with you? Maybe you have been working too much and not getting enough rest. Maybe it's time to carve out time to move your body. Loving and caring for your body, the temple of your soul, is a critical component to experiencing the riches in all areas of your life. When you move your body, you create more movement and flow in your life. Maybe you've recently injured yourself, and you have to take it a little easier. If that is the case, you may also need to take a closer look at the choices you made that led to your injury so that you can "course correct." Whatever it is that you are desiring to experience, you are being guided to focus first on your health.

Home. What's your home like? Is it nice, neat, and organized? Or do you have clutter that's starting to interfere with your healthy and happy environment? Often, when home is someone's entry point, they are needing to clean things up. It may also be time to let go of things. "Out with the old, in with the new!" It can mean that you have been away a lot, and it's time to make sure you spend a little more time at home. You may be wanting a new home, and it may be time to begin taking steps in preparation. If this is your entry point, you probably know why this was identified.

Love. One of my favorites! For many people, this is a calling to open your heart again to experience more love in your life. Maybe, just like the client I referred to earlier, it's time to let the world know you are available. It can also mean that you need to spend more time connecting with your partner or loved one. I recently had someone in my workshop whose eyes got big as saucers. She had been avoiding dating and opening herself to a new relationship since her divorce several years ago. Even though she was a devoted mom and focused on growing her business, she didn't realize how much she was overcompensating for her unexpressed desire to share her life with someone again. The thought of another failed relationship was keeping her from having a healthy and happy relationship that would nourish her heart and soul. Interestingly enough, she kept gaining weight and could not understand what was going on. By squashing her desire of a relationship, her body was overcompensating with the weight.

Family. If this is your entry point, it's possible that you are longing for more connection with your family. Or it could also mean that there is a relationship that needs your attention, possibly addressing something you have been avoiding. It could also mean that you have been focusing your attention elsewhere, maybe on your business, wanting to make certain you are taking good care of your family. Your family, though, really misses and needs you, and you need them. Another person in one of my workshops hadn't realized that this was exactly what was happening with him. His #1 desire was growing his business and increasing his profits. However, his Entry Point was family. He had been focusing so much on his business that he was beginning to neglect his wife and children. I was able to encourage him to structure his time in a way that his family time became a priority. In doing so, he was able to nourish those relationships, but it was also going to nourish him in a way that would allow his business to flow more easily.

Friends/Community. If this is your entry point, it's possible that you have become too isolated and are in need of people that are more like-minded and able to encourage and uplift you. It's possible that you may need to complete a relationship that is no longer serving you. As we grow, our needs and relationships can change. I happen to be a very loyal friend; however, there are times that relationships may have served their purpose. There have been a couple times in my life when I found it necessary to complete a friendship. These are not easy decisions, but they are important ones. It's time to take a closer look at what YOU need and where you may go to better nourish yourself. This Entry Point may also indicate that it may serve you to volunteer for and become involved with an organization. Is there a cause to which you would like to contribute? This is also a great way to meet other people with similar values and interests.

Fun. This one comes up a lot. Unfortunately, there are too many people who have forgotten what it's like to have fun, and they look like they have been blindsided when fun is their Entry Point. If this is the case for you, I suggest you ask people in your life what they do for fun so that you can get new ideas. Then, schedule time in your life to have some fun. Another possibility, although less common, is that you are having too much fun, and you may be neglecting some important tasks. If this is the case, you may want to take a closer look at what may be intimidating about these tasks and why you may be wanting to avoid doing them.

Career/Finance. If this is your Entry Point, the time has come for you to take a closer look at what you want to do with your life. I have seen many examples of people that would really like to start their own business, but they are afraid of letting go of their regular paychecks. In some cases, however, they lose their job and are "forced" to do something new. This is one of the many reasons it becomes important to be honest with yourself and do your part to take steps that best meet your heart's desires, as well as your needs.

If finance is your Entry Point, it may be that you need to take a closer look at your budget and at your spending and savings plans. If these are unknowns, that is a clue that you need to be more conscious about your finances. It could also mean that it's time to invest more in yourself. Have you been wanting to work with a coach, or take a seminar, or even just have a makeover? Do you need some support to help you get where you want to go? We all have blind spots, and we are also not meant to walk this journey in life alone. Take a closer look—an honest one—and listen to what your heart is trying to tell you. Then, follow the pull. It will never let you down!

WORDS OF ENCOURAGEMENT:

Dear God,

I am so grateful to be feeling my deepest desires again. I now realize how I've tried to pretend that it doesn't matter, when now I realize it does. I can see how I've held myself back, trying to make my life "OK," when it hasn't been OK. Please support me with the courage to be honest with myself. Please provide me with the courage and support to do what it takes to make my #1 heart's desire come true because I know if this dream comes true, then all the others will come true more easily as well. Thank you for this wonderful opportunity for me to finally turn my dreams into reality. Thank you for this wonderful opportunity to spread my wings and make my special mark.

Chapter 4

Michelangelo and You

Wendy L. Darling

-4-

Michelangelo and You

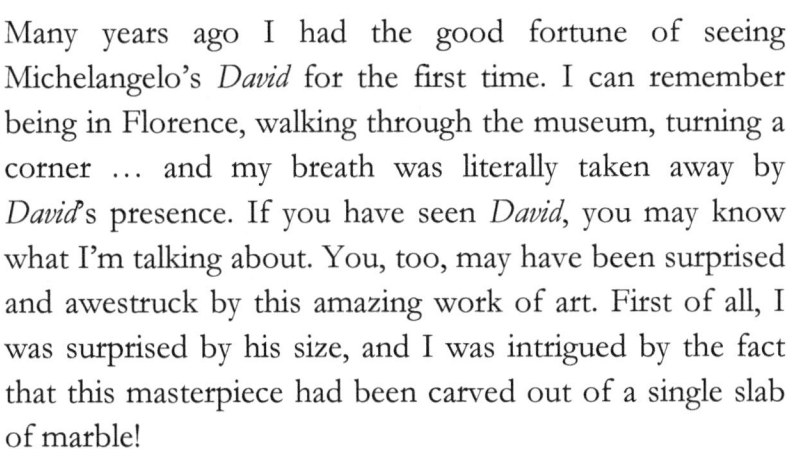

Many years ago I had the good fortune of seeing Michelangelo's *David* for the first time. I can remember being in Florence, walking through the museum, turning a corner ... and my breath was literally taken away by *David*'s presence. If you have seen *David*, you may know what I'm talking about. You, too, may have been surprised and awestruck by this amazing work of art. First of all, I was surprised by his size, and I was intrigued by the fact that this masterpiece had been carved out of a single slab of marble!

Years later, I read an article referencing a time when Michelangelo was supposedly asked that very question: "How were you able to create *David* out of a single slab of marble?"

His response was profound. Michelangelo stated, "*David* already existed within the slab of marble. My job was to simply take away the particles that were NOT *David*!"

And this is my message for YOU! You, too, are a walking masterpiece! One of the reasons you may be sad or confused at this point is that you KNOW there is a better life for you. You KNOW that something is "off" and that you simply have been unable to make the adjustment to live a more authentic life. You have somehow disconnected from and/or overcompensated for being the TRUE YOU, from YOUR unique masterpiece that wants to be expressed. The discomfort you feel is the real you, the TRUE YOU trying to find its way out!

It's time to chisel away the particles that have kept you held back and hidden so that you can spread your wings and make your special mark!

Fortunately for you, I have cracked the code, and I will teach you how to do this.

You MUST believe that your life matters! You MUST believe that you are destined for greatness. And you must believe that the time is NOW for your dreams to come true while you fulfill your life's destiny!

EXERCISE: For a minute, sit with your "magic wand" list. Think about your #1 deepest desire. List the reasons you believe that this has not happened yet. What is the story you keep telling yourself—the reason this has not happened? What shift might be necessary for you to create an opening to welcome this into your life?

WORDS OF ENCOURAGEMENT:

Dear God,

Please allow me to see myself with new eyes. Let me see myself the way you see me. Let me recognize the gifts and special talents I have to offer those in my life. Allow me to recognize how I contribute in my world today, and how I can better contribute to my world tomorrow. Fill me with your love. Allow me to release the hidden particles preventing the real me from emerging. Allow me to spread my wings a little more. Help me find the courage to show the world the real me, the true me, the me you created me to be!

Chapter 5
Where's the Gap

Wendy L. Darling

-5-

Where's the Gap?

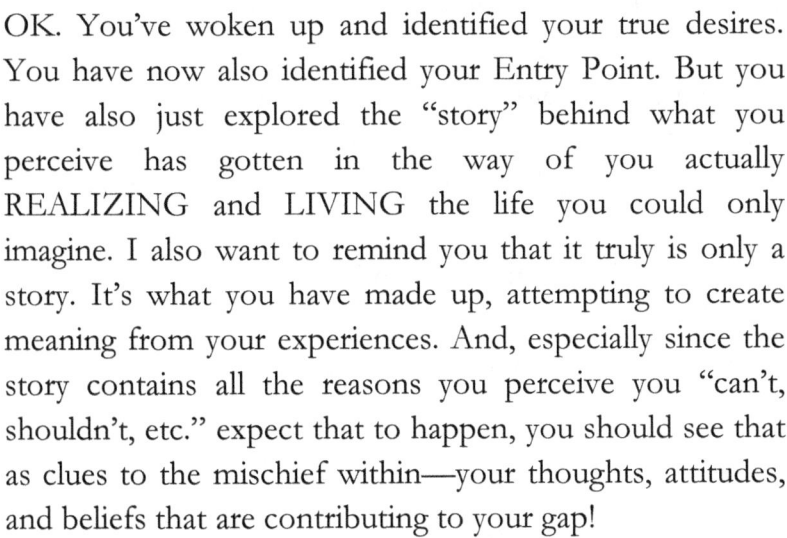

OK. You've woken up and identified your true desires. You have now also identified your Entry Point. But you have also just explored the "story" behind what you perceive has gotten in the way of you actually REALIZING and LIVING the life you could only imagine. I also want to remind you that it truly is only a story. It's what you have made up, attempting to create meaning from your experiences. And, especially since the story contains all the reasons you perceive you "can't, shouldn't, etc." expect that to happen, you should see that as clues to the mischief within—your thoughts, attitudes, and beliefs that are contributing to your gap!

Unfortunately, that also keeps you from taking the steps that would best support you to CLOSE your gap.

So what's a person to do?

WHAT'S OUT OF ALIGNMENT?

First, take a closer look at what may be out of alignment. Maybe your career is going great, but you've neglected your health. Maybe you are dedicating too much time to your work, at your personal expense. Maybe you are overworking because you don't want to go home. Are there issues at home? Is there anyone to go home to?

Take a look at ALL the areas of your life. Look at what's working, where you are satisfied, and where you are not. Most people at this point are very aware of the GAP between where they are and where they want to be.

Unfortunately, this is where many stop. Instead of taking inventory of where they are and where they need to be, their desired results feel more like a gap the size of the Grand Canyon. It then becomes challenging to even imagine being able to accomplish any or most of these items. Thoughts like "How can I?" and "This could never happen to ME" begin to creep in and take over. However, I'm going to help guide you to begin taking those steps. And, little by little, you really are going to be able to close the gap!

I can remember, years ago, when one of my closest friends and I did an exercise similar to this. We created the future we not only desired to experience, but also what we believed was our destiny. When we both finished, we were in awe and delight. However, the next morning, we could barely get our bodies out of bed. The destiny was real, but so was the gap. It truly felt so far away, so unimaginable, that it took the wind out of our sails.

I obviously do not want that to happen to you, so I'm going to suggest how you can begin to take some important steps to move forward.

To begin, take an honest look at where you want to be and where you are now. I want you to fully recognize your gap. It's an important step since it's going to allow you to take a closer look at how you will actually take a step or two to begin moving forward. I don't want you to be overwhelmed, and I certainly don't want you to get stuck. But taking an honest look at yourself, taking this kind of inventory, becomes critically important. Reality can go a very long way in moving you forward.

Not only do you want to be honest about where you want to be, you also need to take a close look at where you are. Part of that is identifying the items and areas where you have NOT been making progress. This tends to represent the mischief-makers of your mind and emotions that create the interference that is holding you back. It may not be the cause, but it certainly is the place you have found to hide out, to hold back, and to prevent you from being in the natural flow of your magnificent life.

Here's a simple way to take inventory and organize yourself:

Where I want to be:	List Your Outcomes
Where I am:	Where you are right now
What's missing or what may be necessary to close the gap:	Initial step(s) to begin

Are there any correlations between what's missing or necessary to close the gap and your Entry Point? If there aren't any obvious correlations, remember to focus on your Entry Point first. THEN, focus on one of the key areas that you have just identified.

Pick the ONE thing that has been an irritant for you, the one thing that if you just experienced a little movement, you would be very happy, and you would feel like you were making some kind of progress. (It may or may not be directly related to your #1 desire.)

MAKING FRIENDS WITH THE GAP

Instead of shutting down with the gap, it's time to find your acceptance and peace with its existence.

It's very healthy to acknowledge where you are and the gap between where you are and where you want to be. This leaning into the gap, this acceptance of it, actually allows for new ideas to flow to you, allowing you to be able to take your next steps.

However, when you allow your mind to go into fear, it will begin creating thoughts like "How can I possibly make this happen?" and "I have no idea what I need to do." It can overwhelm you, and when this happens, it also shuts down the creative force within you that has the ability to guide you each and every step of the way.

It doesn't necessarily mean you won't need help and support, but you will begin to recognize when you need to reach out for help. It will also help you see where you need to put more effort in taking another step, whatever that may be for you.

MOVEMENT, taking action, being willing to take another step—these all have wonderful effects on receiving creative, strategic steps on your path to fulfilling your Divine Destiny. And God and the Universe reward ACTION! It's just that simple.

You don't have to take a bunch of steps, but as you begin to move, you will find your energy and momentum begin to build, and each step gets easier and easier.

There will still be moments when you get caught up in worry and fear, but you will recognize these moments more easily, and in later chapters I'll guide you and help you see what you can do when you hit these roadblocks.

Wendy L. Darling

WORDS OF ENCOURAGEMENT:

Dear God,

I am beginning to awaken and FEEL the truth of who I am. I am so grateful for this miraculous life and opportunity you have provided for me. I am grateful that I am able to begin recognizing all that you have been attempting to get me to see, recognize, and experience. Continue to guide me, love me, and support me. Help me hear the gentle whispers, the messages, the courage, and the assurance that I am, in fact, taking the best steps for me. I am forever grateful that I now realize how blessed I am. I dedicate myself to spending time each day with you. Thank you for all that you continue to do for me, allowing me to recognize and appreciate the miracle that is my life, the blessings of my journey.

Wendy L. Darling

Chapter 6

The Positioning and Driving Forces of Your Values

Wendy L. Darling

-6-

The Positioning and Driving Forces of Your Values

You've continued your journey of uncovering your deepest desires, your Divine Design and Destiny. You know where you want to be and you are clear on the gap that exists. Now we need to put this in motion. We're going to go deeper. We are going to examine your values.

Your values are what POSITION you to be in alignment so that you are able to take the actions that best support your efforts. You values are your engine. It's where all that is important to you and your life are categorized and stored. By taking another honest look at yourself and what is most important to you, you will be able to position yourself to live a much more authentic life, one that is in full alignment with your truth, your mission, your purpose, your Divine Design and Destiny.

It's important to add this component to your Divine Design and Destiny equation because this is the motor, the positioning that is required for you to be in alignment with your TRUTH. Without conscious awareness, you can inadvertently take actions that are misaligned with what is most important to you. When you face challenges moving forward, one reason may be there is a conflict within your values system. For the "machine of your life" to be operating correctly, you must have alignment. And with early conditioning and the other "shoulds" that we tend to inadvertently integrate, there is a tendency to create issues that prevent your machine from operating effectively and with ease.

For example, you may want to experience successful growth in your business, but time with your family is a high value. These are both excellent values; however, if not examined closely, there can be a conflict interfering in both areas. I just want you to be in alignment with what you are destined to create and experience. By taking a closer look, you can make some simple adjustments to alleviate any conflicts or misalignments, if there are any.

As with the example above, you may just need to make a conscious decision that no matter what, you end your workday by a particular time, ensuring you spend quality time with your family.

I used to make sure I got home by a certain time when my son was young, and I scooped up that time, enjoying it to the max. Then, after he was in bed, I may have found it necessary to spend a little time with my work.

Since my health is very important, I also had to find creative ways to get in some exercise time. When my son was young, the best time for me was taking a quick break at lunch. At that time, I had a gym in the building where I worked, making that a simple solution. Even though it's now many years later, I still find that taking a midday break works best for me.

There were many years I got up at 5:30 a.m. to make sure I got in that workout, but I'm grateful that I can now adjust that to a time that better suits my current lifestyle. One of the reasons that this better supports me is that I now find it important to spend my first moments in quiet meditation. When I begin my day this way, I find I am truly in the magnificent flow of my life.

So let's have you take a closer look at your values. Your values create your core foundation and are also one of the driving forces that propel you into action. Your values get you out of bed in the morning and help you take steps that are not necessarily comfortable. Your values fuel your determination to move forward and push you out of your own way and out of your comfort zone. They also keep you on track, honest, and living your life with integrity (all of which are fundamental values).

EXERCISE: Take a look at the following list and check those values that are important to you. This is not a complete list, but it will at least get you started. (For a more complete list, go to http://wendydarling.com/book-bonuses/

Acceptance	Desire	Motivation
Achievement	Determination	Optimism
Acknowledgement	Discipline	Organization
Adaptability	Effectiveness	Originality
Ambition	Endurance	Passion
Appreciation	Energy	Peacefulness
Awareness	Enjoyment	Proficiency
Balance	Enthusiasm	Professionalism
Beauty	Fairness	Prosperity
Belongingness	Faith	Reliability
Brilliance	Fame	Selflessness
Calmness	Focus	Self-realization
Camaraderie	Freedom	Sensitivity
Certainty	Generosity	Spirituality
Clarity	Gentility	Spontaneity
Comfort	Genuineness	Success
Commitment	Gratitude	Teamwork
Compassion	Happiness	Timeliness
Competence	Harmony	Trust
Confidence	Health	Truth
Conformity	Honesty	Uniqueness
Congruency	Impact	Virtue
Connection	Integrity	Vision
Consciousness	Intuition	Vitality
Cooperation	Leadership	Wealth
Courage	Love	Wisdom
Credibility	Loyalty	
Dependability	Mastery	

Next, I want you to go through the list again, choosing the top 10-15 values that are MOST important to you.

With your final list, I want you to take each value and place them in one of the following categories:

The values that support my intention. An intention is something you INTEND to do, feel, experience, create, ACCOMPLISH. It's your first position when targeting a desired result.

The values that support my movement: These are the values that support movement for your desired results. These get your motor going and get you into action.

The values for road blocks and blind spots: What values are important to you when you hit a stumbling block, when you've hit the wall, etc.? What do you need within you to help you assess, reposition, and reboot?

Values for fulfillment: What values do you want to be present as you experience the fruits of your labor?

THE VALUES THAT SUPPORT MY INTENTION	
THE VALUES THAT SUPPORT MY MOVEMENT	
THE VALUES FOR ROADBLOCKS AND BLIND SPOTS	
VALUES FOR FULFILLMENT	

This is going to help you process not only how you want to FEEL, but what is going to be positioned within your core. This will help you make decisions and begin to take steps to move forward, especially in more challenging times. They will also help you recognize and celebrate your progress and successes.

To drive this home even further, I want you now to create a **DECLARATION OF DIVINE DESTINY!**

Declaration of Divine Destiny

What is a declaration of divine destiny? It's a bold statement, a proclamation that literally declares who you are, what you stand for, and the "space" you are committed to holding, allowing your Divine Destiny to unfold.

What is the purpose? The purpose is to position you to hold the thoughts, the emotions, and the energy that will catapult you forward. When you FEEL your declaration, you BECOME your declaration, inviting all your guidance and direction to freely come to you. AND you are also able to take your steps with greater ease.

Now let's begin creating your statement.

First, look at your list of core values in each category. From each category, choose ONE value that is most critical for you. If that seems impossible, choose no more than two. These are to be the MOST important values, ones that you cannot live without—you can't imagine life without them. Period.

If you have difficulty making those decisions, you can do the following "forced-choice" decision-making exercise.

Let's say your top two intention values are generating a steady flow of income and having a significant impact. Using the forced-choice process, would it be better to have a steady flow of cash or to create a significant impact?

In my world, having a significant impact is key. If I am making a significant impact, money is no longer an issue. AND the money flows as I'm making an impact.

Having optimal health may be next on your list. Which is more important: optimal health or creating a significant impact?

Again, in my world, creating optimal health is important, otherwise I risk not being able to make a significant impact.

Now let's look at your next value. Let's say that is courage. Since you have now identified that health is number one, how does that compare to having courage? If health still remains number one, then you can also compare it to your number-two value, which in this example is making a significant impact.

Continue examining the other values on your list until you have identified your number-one value.

Do this for the other three categories. When you are done, you will have four to eight values.

Next, I want you to take your four to eight values and create a declaration, a proclamation of who you are going to be, your commitment to how you are going to feel, and your determination for fulfillment, what you will be doing, and the results and impact you will be experiencing.

For example, your Declaration of Divine Destiny could be:

By nourishing my health and well-being, receiving the love and support from my Beloved, my family and friends, I provide a platform for clarity, focus, and direction, guiding those I serve to have rich, miraculous lives, while they have greater impact and fulfill their Divine Design and Destiny.

Remember, the purpose of this exercise is to help POSITION you from the inside so that you can create and achieve your desired results on the outside. There is no right or wrong way. This is to be used as a reminder and inspiration for you to continue moving forward.

Wendy L. Darling

WORDS OF ENCOURAGEMENT:

Dear God,

I am forever grateful for this wonderful life you have bestowed upon me. I am grateful for the opportunity to blossom into my truth and live this miraculous life. Help me find my clarity, my center, my knowing of who I am and the life I am destined to live. Fill me with your love, guide me along the way, and provide me with the support that continues to nourish me along this magnificent journey. I am forever grateful for my magical, miraculous life.

Chapter 7

Good Vibrations – It's All About Energy!

Wendy L. Darling

-7-

Good Vibrations – It's All About Energy!

OK, let's keep going.

Remember how I mentioned that I used to be a management and organizational development consultant? I also received two graduate degrees in counseling psychology and completed post-graduate work in management and organizational development. However, after my accident, my life took a significant turn in MANY ways.

You already know the heartaches that occurred with my family.

Now I'm about to tell you how things began changing for the GOOD.

After losing custody of my son, I was broken in a million pieces, maybe more. I was still fragile from my accident and simply didn't have the reserves to deal with this shock. I never imagined this would happen. Shortly after, my mom suggested that I might benefit from meditation.

At that time, "quieting my mind" was an oxymoron. I had NO idea how that could even be possible. For such a long time, my mind had been spinning like a hamster on a wheel, and I literally could not shut it off. It was searching for a reason to explain why something this horrific had happened to me, and there were no "files" in my mind to explain this.

So being in a horrible state and suffering beyond measure, I was willing to try anything that might help alleviate my pain. I reached out to someone to teach me. I was with a small group of others who were learning the art of meditation. I clearly remember the night everything changed.

We were all sitting in separate places in someone's home. As I sat there practicing, I ALMOST felt like my mind was going to relax, and each time I had this feeling, I kept feeling an urge to sing. It was a rather peculiar feeling. I kept pushing it aside and focusing on my breath, but it simply would not go away. I mentioned this to the person who was guiding me, and he simply said, "So sing!" I also remember my response. "You don't understand," I chuckled. "I actually have people in my life who request I

NOT do that!" After a brief pause, he responded once again, "So sing."

And I did.

It wasn't Top 40 kind of singing. It was melodic and very calming. In fact, my mind and body immediately relaxed! What a RELIEF!

When I opened my eyes, the other people in the group had come over, amazed by what they had heard. I was embarrassed, not realizing that they were wondering what I had done—AND they liked what they had heard.

At least all of this encouraged me to continue.

I had set up a little meditation space in my walk-in closet, so now I was (literally) a closet singer. Within a short amount of time, I began relaxing my mind, while relaxing into my body and my life. I'm not sure any other kind of medicine could have soothed me the way this worked for me.

Then one day, another life-changing moment occurred.

One of my son's friends had gotten sick while she was playing at our house. I had put her in my bed, and after a while, I went upstairs to check on her. While talking to her, I had this very sudden and strong urge to sing to her. I mentioned this to her, and she said she'd like me to do that, so I did. Within minutes, she was completely well!

I remember her looking up at me with such a sweet and special smile. She asked, "How did you do that?" Well, since I had NO idea what had just happened, I was dancing with my thoughts and words. I ended up saying to her, "I believe you wanted to get well, and God heard your request, so he sent his love through me for you to get well." She smiled and simply said, "Cool!"

Meanwhile, my mind was going a little "wonky." What had just happened? How could that have really happened? And that was the beginning of the next phase of discovering how energy influences our bodies and all other aspects of our lives.

So I started to play, and over the years I have learned how to master energy for myself, and now with others. This is what I am about to teach you.

At times, this may seem a bit far-fetched. It certainly took a long time for me to feel comfortable with what I was now capable of offering. However, I have come to realize what an extraordinary gift I received from such a challenging time in my life.

And THIS is the gift that keeps on giving because I believe I was chosen to help you to live the life you were designed to live. And THAT is an honor I cherish each and every day.

We're going to break down this system, piece by piece. I'm going to show you how your vision, your mind, and your feelings all contribute to your unique energy system. Then we're going to tie it all together to position you to walk your remaining days living your Divine Destiny.

I am going to do my best to help you understand how this all works. It is a very unique blend of the energy of the mind, the heart, and the body that allows you to lean into and embrace your unique signature, your unique brand, your unique Divine Design and Destiny so that you can live your unique, miraculous life!

EXERCISE: To begin to explore how energy impacts your life today, think of a time that you were really happy. What was going on? How did you FEEL? On a scale of 1–10, with 10 meaning you feel fantastically energized, in a positive sense, and 1 meaning you feel blah, or in a negative sense, what number would you give this experience?

Now think of a time that you were really sad or angry or frustrated. How did that make you feel? On a scale of 1–10, how energetic did you feel? Now take inventory of how you FEEL right now. What is going on that is contributing to the rating you gave yourself? What might you imagine that could allow you to shift to a higher number (if you were below a 10)? The shift is possible. It's also important. This is where we are going to focus so that you can learn how to strengthen.

WORDS OF ENCOURAGEMENT:

Dear God,

I am so very grateful for beginning to see how I have kept you out of my life. I can see how I have pushed you away and all the good you have been trying to bring to me. Help me relax into the comfort of your love. Help me to FEEL you throughout my whole body. Help me feel you showering me with your presence. Help me feel the gratitude for this magnificent life and opportunity you have provided for me.

Chapter 8

The Value of Your Vision

Wendy L. Darling

-8-

The Value of Your Vision

There is a common phrase that says, "If you can see it, you can be it!" To a certain extent, I believe that as well. Unfortunately for me, my inner ability to visualize is one of the areas of my brain that was affected by my accident. But, at least for me, it gave me the opportunity to develop my other senses and design a more complete system to help you materialize YOUR desires.

It also made me realize that many other people also have difficulty visualizing their heart's desires, especially if it seems like there is a huge gap—something unimaginable, even unattainable. The larger the gap between your desire and reality, the more challenging it may be for you to visualize and to integrate your vision into your mind and heart. So I learned how to jump-start it all and combine these components into one sweet little package.

Now, let's go back to your deepest desires. How would you and your life be impacted if you lived this way? I know a lot of people think that if they won the lottery, this would change everything! In many ways, it would. But I want you to live and experience life as if you have just won the lottery of life. That can be and IS your destiny!

YOUR DIVINE DESIGN AND DESTINY BOARD

One of the easiest ways to begin is to create a Divine Design and Destiny Board, which is different from a vision board.

I know vision boards are very common, but I want this exercise to be an intuitive experience, not a mental one. I want this to be an experience from your heart and your heart's desires. I want you to really dig deep and bring to life your divine design. In my opinion, vision boards do tend to be a visual representation of the desires you wish to experience in your life. However, I want you to go deeper and really get in touch with your deepest desires because I believe they are indicators of your Divine Destiny.

I don't want these to just be wishes. I want these to be your deepest desires, because your deepest desires are your TRUTH. It's part of your Divine Destiny blueprint.

The reason it's important to find pictures to represent them is that this is how your brain can best be programmed to receive messages. And when your mind is constantly receiving messages, it also is constantly working with the Universe to find ways to make that happen.

I also know that for many, me included, internally visualizing these images can be challenging, especially when a gap is involved. That's why this can be a great way to jump-start the battery needed to get your mind and emotions supporting you and working for you.

I believe each and every one of us has a blueprint, of sorts, within our DNA that has our Divine Design and Destiny encoded. I believe that your destiny is predetermined. You are encoded with your gifts, your mission and purpose, and a variety of paths you could take, all leading to the same destination. It's a "homing device" of a wonderful kind. And as we become more aware of this, the miracles and magic of life continue to unfold.

In my world, I can imagine sitting in God's lap as a soul, soon to embark to this place known as "Earth school." At that time, you and God review where you have been and how you may wish to evolve. And in God's wonderful way, he smiles and basically says, "Wish granted." For example, maybe your next evolution is to experience unconditional love in a way that you have never experienced before, so God smiles at you and, of course, puts everything in motion to fulfill your next round of "Earth school."

But here is where it can get interesting. Maybe you were put in a family where there was a contrast to unconditional love. Maybe you had parents that were critical, possibly even abusive. You started from a challenging place, but you now have the opportunity to go down a path to grow and evolve into an amazing person, one who exhibits and lives as a truly unconditional loving person. In doing so, you are able to contribute to others in ways you never could imagine possible. You now are able to extend a helping hand, with love and a deep sense of compassion. You can now not only offer inspiration, but a direction others can follow.

How many stories have you heard about the miracles that arise from adversity? I'm sure you have a story to tell as well.

The reason I want you to have these visual representations of your Divine Design and Destiny is I want you to KNOW in your heart of hearts that this is your TRUTH. These are not wishes; these are not airy-fairy hopes and dreams. This is your reality that has been calling you, waiting for you, and now opening you to receive guidance and direction.

Every time you look at your Divine Design and Destiny Board, you will not only keep all your TRUTHS alive, you will be constantly reminded that these ARE your truths!

From this day forward I want you to be living in a state of CERTAINTY.

EXERCISE: Gather up your magazines, or go out and buy a few. Now begin looking at the pages and cut out pictures and words that you feel represent the future you are now creating for yourself. It's good to "just do it"—don't put meaning to any of it. If you are drawn to a picture of a colorful flower, cut it out. If a word jumps off the page, cut the word out. If there is something specific that you know needs to be on your board, yet you haven't found a picture that represents that, Google Images can come to the rescue. Just Google what you may be looking for and see the wide variety of options in front of you.

I like to think these are guided moments and a wonderful way for you to strengthen your intuition, what I refer to as your internal guidance system.

Your internal guidance system is a divinely guided GPS that has your best interest at heart, that has your Divine Design and Destiny programmed in, and that is constantly looking out for you, guiding you. When you have cultivated this connection, in my opinion, you have EVERYTHING. Worries no longer exist because you know you are safe and your best interests are being taken care of. Your job is to pay attention and take a step when guided.

So, as a starting point, this exercise can help you wake up and strengthen that connection.

Spend time going through at least four or five magazines. Once you are done, we'll take it a step farther and create your Divine Design and Destiny Board.

Get a poster board and some glue. Again, I want this to be an intuitive experience. See where a picture or word wants to be placed on the page. Allow your pictures and words to naturally be drawn to a special place on your board. Allow your inner guidance system to lead the way. Although you may now not use all your pictures and words, trust that you will have just the right pictures and words to create the cues that best support this next phase of your life. I also happen to use the Feng Shui Bagua. Because of how my mind works, it's easier for me to categorize and organize. You can Google this as well, if you are interested.

I like this process to not only be a representation of my Divine Design and Destiny, but also to be messages from my higher wisdom, my soul, my guidance. When I arrange my pictures and words in this way, I am always in awe of what the final "product" looks like. As I look at this each and every day, I am reminded of my truth, my direction, and my destiny. I also feel my resolve and determination well up within me to take my next step(s), whatever they may be. I may not always achieve my destinations with a certain timeframe, but once I complete most of what was on my board, I create a new one. However, many times creating a Divine Design and Destiny Board has become my ritual of welcoming in a new year.

Why is it important to keep creating a new board? Because it is also important to make sure you continue to grow and evolve!

The importance of having a Divine Design and Destiny board is that you need to strengthen your mind, your heart, and your personal energy system. You need to have your mind and emotions working FOR you. When the mind is shown pictures, it begins to go to work to find solutions to make that happen. And, as you raise your energetic vibration through these mechanisms, that's when the magic really starts happening. It is not only important that you SEE your desires turning into reality, but it's also important to believe it and feel it as well.

WORDS OF ENCOURAGEMENT:

Dear God,

I thank you for the amazing blessings in my life. I thank you for providing me with such a special vision of how my life is to be. I know it seems impossible for me to realize, but now I surrender and allow you to show me the way. Please help me continue to see this reality. Please help me KNOW in my heart of hearts that this is my truth. Help me sustain the courage, the insights, and the strength to continue to move forward. Thank you for this beautiful life you have provided for me. I pledge to continue to walk in faith and in honor of the life with which you have blessed me.

Chapter 9

The Magic of Your Mind

Wendy L. Darling

-9-

The Magic of Your Mind

We are barely scratching the surface, beginning to understand and appreciate how the mind works. It will be very clear that I am NOT a scientist, but I do read a fair amount about how the brain functions and how it impacts your choices, your feelings, your actions, and your results.

If you want to get an idea of how your mind is currently supporting you, just take a closer look at your life. To what extent are you living the life of your desires? Do you want that healthy, lean, and fit body? Look in the mirror and tell me if it looks like that. Do you want that amazing relationship? Is he or she in your life? How's your career going? Your finances? OK, you hopefully are getting an idea of the point I'm trying to make.

The way your mind works—its job, in part—is to keep you safe and "support" you in creating your reality. However, your internal reality may not be in alignment with the life of your desires. If there is a GAP between your desires and your Divine Destiny, you are now seeing how your mind is working for you, or possibly against what you desire.

It is estimated that we have between 60,000 and 70,000 thoughts in a day! It is also estimated that the majority of those thoughts are the very same ones you had the day before. With all your past experiences, neural pathways have been created, which are the highways of your thoughts, which, when repeated over and over again, form your beliefs and habits. And what is even more unfortunate, these beliefs and habits are SO ingrained within you, they are such a natural and familiar part of you, that they are more than likely operating on a subconscious level. That means that you are not even AWARE of how your mind is operating and impacting your actions.

All of those thoughts that are floating around inside you are directly impacting your unique ENERGY SYSTEM! Happy thoughts have a higher vibrational frequency than negative ones, and these same thoughts are directly impacting your feelings, choices, and actions.

Have you ever walked into a room and you could just tell which people you were drawn to speak with and those that you wanted to avoid? Have you ever felt really wonderful, but then after speaking to someone for a while, your energy felt much lower, as if you had just been slimed?

I'm not trying to be cruel. I have great compassion for people who are struggling with themselves and their lives. I have also learned how to guard myself during those conversations. In fact, I have learned how to transform them during the conversations. And, because of the way my mind, emotions, and energy systems operate today, not many of those people even come into my life.

Getting back to your mind.

So what's happening to those 60,000-plus thoughts each day? Thousands and thousands of thoughts are "talking," making commands, and you don't even know they are because they are not in your conscious awareness.

How does that happen?

I'll try to explain it in simple terms.

When you are first born, you begin FEELING different experiences since you do not have words yet to describe your experiences. However, as you learn language, these feelings become thoughts that get filed in your mind. The more you have the thought, the stronger the thoughts become. Then they are grouped into different files, classifications, such as "I'm safe," "I'm not safe," and "Love." The more frequently these thoughts are accessed and experienced, you create neural pathways in your mind that are constantly being activated.

An example I use all the time is when you make a decision to eat healthier, to exercise, and to shed yourself of a few extra pounds. Sunday you have your "last hoorah" meal, go to the grocery store, stock up on healthy food, and promise that you are going to the gym first thing in the morning. And maybe you do. But after a while, other foods begin to call your name, and other activities get in the way of getting your exercise in.

You definitely and consciously WANT to shed those extra pounds, but your subconscious programming keeps you "safe" in your comfort zone. Somewhere along the way, you programmed your mind to believe that it wasn't safe for you to be healthy, lean, and fit, and/or your mind doesn't believe you are worthy of being healthy, lean, and fit. Maybe you learned ways to punish yourself, and this is the way to keep that belief alive.

You may also do the same with your relationships, your career, and your finances.

The good news is that we now have ways to quiet the subconscious mind and create NEW, empowering thoughts and new neural pathways!! Isn't that great?

We are able to access your inaccurate, faulty programming of your mind and heart that is getting in the way of you experiencing EVERYTHING you have ever dreamed of for your life! Not only can you rid yourself of its influence, you are now able to program a new, empowering thought that better supports you.

It may take a little time; it may not. But your life can change once you begin implementing the Healing Harmonics™ System where you unleash your signature Divine Destiny.

EXERCISE: Of your desires, which one is #1? Write out all the thoughts that you have about this. Really go for all the negative thoughts that you may be having. What would someone be thinking who wasn't living their Divine Destiny? What thoughts would someone have if they deeply wanted a relationship, a healthy body, or to be financially free, but never could make that happen?

Now, for each negative statement, write out the opposite, a positive one, because these are the thoughts that you are now going to need to program into your mind. At first, these may not seem real, but with time you will be able to integrate them so that they feel natural to you.

Negative thoughts:

_____
_____
_____
_____
_____

Your Divine Destiny thoughts:

_____
_____
_____
_____
_____
_____
_____

WORDS OF ENCOURAGEMENT:

Dear God,

You have gifted me with a brilliant mind. Please help guide me to strengthen my mind to represent the truth of who I am. Please allow me to find ways to easily shift my mind to begin celebrating my life. Help me know my mind is my new best friend, allowing it to better support me. With time, I know it will feel empowered to make the magic it was designed to do. Thank you for my amazing, miraculous mind.

Wendy L. Darling

Chapter 10

The Power of Your Heart

Wendy L. Darling

-10-

The Power of Your Heart

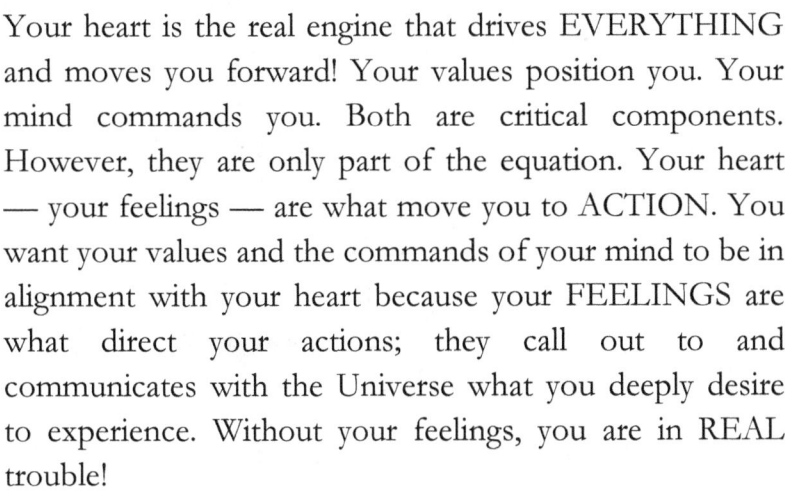

Your heart is the real engine that drives EVERYTHING and moves you forward! Your values position you. Your mind commands you. Both are critical components. However, they are only part of the equation. Your heart — your feelings — are what move you to ACTION. You want your values and the commands of your mind to be in alignment with your heart because your FEELINGS are what direct your actions; they call out to and communicates with the Universe what you deeply desire to experience. Without your feelings, you are in REAL trouble!

Many people have done a very good job of squashing their feelings after heartache and disappointments, or simply out of sheer exhaustion, trying very hard to make life work. Because of this, your thoughts can help stoke the fire of your feelings, or they can do a very good job of putting out the very flames of the feelings that are needed!

So what's a person to do?

It's important to take regular "time-outs" to make certain that you are FEELING positive, loving feelings. I know that it may be impossible to feel that way 24/7, but it can also be a lofty goal to shoot for. It doesn't mean that you have to FEEL ecstatic each and every moment. It means you need to do your best to feel authentic, calm, and loving. These are all gentle feelings that require little of your energy. In fact, it takes far less energy to feel this way than it does to feel the negative ones. Even worse, it takes a lot of energy to keep the feelings you never allowed yourself to experience pushed down and locked away, stored inside your body.

Something that can help you better navigate your feelings throughout the day is to set your phone alarm to go off on the hour to allow you to walk around, shake out your body, and take some really deep breaths, which allows love to flow through you. It's a way to replenish and renew yourself during the day.

In his book *Power vs. Force*, David Hawkins shared his results of a thirty-year study. He investigated, researched, and measured a variety of emotions and was able then to equate them to vibrational frequencies. The emotions of hate, disgust, frustration, sadness, etc. were found to have a lower vibrational frequency. Happiness, joy, and love had a higher vibrational frequency. He actually created a scale showing his results. What this means is that the good emotions created more positive energy, and the not-so-good ones created a heavier, lower energy.

But this is the part that I personally loved the best.

His findings concluded that when a person vibrates at a higher level of frequency, it can override the lower-level ones. Consider someone who is having a bad day. I can remember being in a restaurant and our server seemed tired, overworked, and distracted. We decided to take a moment and send him some love. What that means is I felt love, then, with intention, I sent him my love. You can do this with your feelings alone, or saying 'I love you,' while feeling love. When he returned in a couple minutes, he was like a new person and a great waiter!

I speak at high schools and leadership conferences, and I demonstrate the power of your feelings. I have an exercise that shows how a positive emotion overrides a negative one. It's rather eye-opening.

I teach our youth that the people that are walking around their schools labeled as bullies or troublemakers are merely people who have had their hearts stomped on. They have little to no love in their "love well," and this is the best they know how to be to survive. I show the students how they can send love to these people and fill up their love tanks without them ever knowing! Change can actually happen that easily. How cool is that? Not only am I teaching these kids to look beyond the surface, but they are also learning they can easily have a positive impact on their lives and the lives of others.

This is an important message for you, as well. You can begin changing your internal landscape by learning how to infuse more love into your body and system. And when your "love well" is filled, you can offer more love to others.

EXERCISE: Before you begin worrying about helping others, this is an exercise that will help you fill YOUR love tank. Depending on your life, your day, and your circumstances, you will benefit from doing this at least once a day. It's a great practice to do first thing in the morning, and as you lie in bed at night, it's a great exercise to complete your day.

Close your eyes and imagine you are surrounded in a "shield" of love. Take a moment to see your body literally encapsulated in a shield of armor—only this is your love armor. Nothing negative can come inside you. Now imagine the heavens showering you with love. It may seem sparkly, or it may resemble a flowing stream. It's your vision, so you get to decide. Allow this love energy to flow through you and around you, filling you up. See it begin at the top of your head and flow through all parts of your body. Allow any excess to come out of your feet, into the ground. This is also a great exercise for cleaning your energy field of any negative energy you may have picked up during your day. Repeat the same practice at night.

Words of Encouragement:

Dear God,

I thank you for giving me such an amazing, generous heart. I am so grateful for all I can feel, all that I am able to experience. Please allow your love to wash away the heartaches from my past. Please allow your love to flow through me, washing away anything that is not true to who I am. Please continue to strengthen me, to find the courage to feel deeply, and please allow me to feel the gentle pull so that I can echo to the world my unique heart song. I am forever grateful for my magnificent heart.

Chapter 11

Your Body Is the Temple for Your Soul

Wendy L. Darling

-11-

Your Body Is the Temple for Your Soul

———≈———

We've been given this amazing opportunity called "life," yet how do you care for your body? It's one thing to focus on the mind and the heart, but if you are neglecting your sweet body, you are at risk of not fulfilling your Divine Destiny.

Unfortunately, in our busy lives, it's too easy to place the importance of caring for your body last on the list. I know your life may be busy, but can you really afford NOT to take care of yourself? And if you have children, what are you teaching them?

Our bodies are like newborn babies. They are totally dependent upon us to provide and care for them. Have you ever thought about your body that way?

It's doing the best it can, given (literally) what it's given. When you feed your body with food that nourishes and supports it, it's able to do its job easily. It wants to be healthy. It wants YOU to be healthy! That's its job! But when you feed it food that makes it work harder, you're making your body's job even harder.

When you don't drink enough water (and your body is made up mainly of water), again, it's harder for it to function.

It also needs movement and additional oxygen, which makes getting different types of exercise critical for your body to maintain optimal health and performance.

Just as your thoughts and feelings put out a vibrational frequency, your thoughts and feelings also directly impact your body. Your body is obviously a critical component, your vehicle for assisting you to live and experience your Divine Design and Destiny.

Is your body shouting out to the heavens, "We're doing it!" or is it calling out, "I can't keep going on like this"? No body, no life. How might you be taking that sweet body of yours for granted?

The choice is yours.

I know I love certain foods, and I continue to eat them. However, an act of love for me is choosing foods on a regular basis that support my body. I make certain that I get liquids in my body on a fairly regular basis, and I also make an effort to move and strengthen my body. In fact, I went for quite a while without exercise, and I saw how my body started to change. I had gone through a rough patch, and without even realizing it, I had dropped out of regular exercise. For me, this is one of the very top factors that contribute to my health, wealth, and love life!

No matter what your choices have been in the past, no matter what state your body may be in right now, it's a new day. You can make better choices.

What might you be able to do to improve your health and take better care of your body?

EXERCISE: Make a list of things that you could do that represent taking better care of your body. Is it drinking more water? Eating foods that better nourish your body? Getting more exercise? Is there ONE activity that you can begin doing NOW that can move you in the direction demonstrating to your body "I love you and I am taking good care of you"? Take that step. And tomorrow, take another! You have been given only one body, so please cherish it and make the most of it. Our time on Earth really is precious. Your body is the one thing in your life over which you have direct control and impact.

Wendy L. Darling

WORDS OF ENCOURAGEMENT:

Dear God,

I am so grateful for this amazing body with which you gifted me. I am saddened by how I have forgotten how precious this sweet body of mine is. Please help me find forgiveness in my heart for how I have treated my body, neglected it, and not properly loved and cared for it. Allow me now to remember that I have been given this precious life, and my body is the vehicle you provided for me to experience all that you have in store for me. Help me properly nourish my body. Help me move my body in a variety of ways each and every day. And, most important, help me to remember to thank my body for such a magnificent job it provides each and every day of my life. I am truly grateful for the gift my body provides.

Chapter 12

Focus on MEE

Wendy L. Darling

-12-

Focus on MEE

(mind, emotions, energy)

---≈---

"I was so worried about you – I forgot about me"

It is all too common to focus our attention on others and outside responsibilities, making it easy to forget that you are the captain of your ship. With your hands on the wheel, you are steering "your life" in the direction you want to head. However, too often we turn the wheel over to another person—a spouse, a child, a friend, a boss, a coworker—and suddenly we're wondering what's going on. In many ways, it's wonderful to be generous. However, you first have to focus on yourself so that you then can put your energies on others and your other responsibilities.

Giving and being of service is an excellent quality to possess. However, I have also found the more generous a person is, the less they tend to focus on themselves. Yes, there are psychological reasons that this has probably happened, but we won't bother to get into that. Just know that if you are an over-giver, you may have a weaker "receiving" muscle, and you may be putting yourself at risk because you are neglecting your own needs.

I do NOT want to diminish the concept of contributing and being of service. However, there is a critical foundational component that needs to be addressed to allow you to maximize the results you want to experience and achieve.

That is the concept of putting YOUR oxygen mask on first.

Most of us have been on at least one airplane and have heard the genius: *"If, in the rare circumstance of an emergency and the use of oxygen is needed, it is important, if travelling with a child or a person who may require your assistance, to place your oxygen mask on first. Then assist them."*

I hope you can appreciate the importance of this message. If you are not taking care of yourself, how can you possibly believe that you will be able to take care of others?

I can remember the first talk I gave when I addressed this very topic. It was for a group of professors at a university.

My presentation discussed how they could be more effective in their roles, and burnout was becoming more common for them and their staff.

When I shared this with them—as I am with you right now—the concept of putting your oxygen mask on first, I could see that this was not the most comfortable conversation. I remember the silence of the room and their attention, as if this was a new concept they had never heard or considered before.

"It is very clear that you offer your skills, your gifts, and your talents generously. And you serve a wonderful purpose in preparing our youth for their future. However, if you do not take time for YOU, what good will you ultimately be for another? The good news is that you have the skills. All you have to do is begin applying those skills to yourself."

I remember feeling the wheels of their minds turning in that moment of silence. I could tell it had not even occurred to them that they could do this.

You DO have the skills to serve, and you must use those very skills to serve yourself first. If this is true for you, I encourage you look at what is keeping you from putting your oxygen mask on first.

FOCUS ON "MEE" – MIND, EMOTIONS, ENERGY

To bring into focus how you can leverage yourself with greater ease, let's examine some of the clues that can possibly shed some light on ways you may be holding yourself back and how you can position yourself with what really matters to you.

1. **Do your know your gifts, your personal brilliance, your genius?** If you are not sure, which is also common, let me suggest a couple ways to help you identify this. Gifts come in different packages. One is that certain things come really easy to you. It's effortless. It's just the way you think, act, and behave. For example, I am really good at finding other people's gifts. It's just easy for me to spot that. I'm also really good at finding the "niggle," the root cause of what's creating a misalignment within you. Even though I have a comprehensive diagnostic system in place, I actually can do this intuitively. And, unfortunately, many times your gift is so natural to who you are, you may not even realize it's something special.

Second, ask your family and friends. What is it that they value about you? What do they appreciate about you? What do they perceive you are good at? It wasn't until one of my professors pointed out to me how good I was with diagnostics that I realized this was something that came easy to me, but not necessarily to other people.

I can also remember a time when I saw one of my son's gifts. He was given a computer game as a gift. It was one of those more violent, fighting types of games. I did not like it—and he loved it. It was probably one of the few places where we disagreed since I didn't want him playing this game, much less spending so much time playing it.

Then one evening, he showed me what he had done. He had filmed one of the "battles" and put music to it. I was amazed at how it changed my whole experience of his game. It was clear this was one of his gifts. He even turned my negative attitude about his game into a positive one. By infusing a different style of music that didn't actually match the action, it completely changed the impact of what I was watching. It was rather amazing.

My son later got into film production and editing, and was able to utilize his gifts.

The reason this is important is that if you are not nourishing your gifts, if you're not expressing them in some way, it is going to cause your energy to deplete.

2. **Do you know what makes your heart sing?** These provide additional clues for you. What moves you when you watch a movie? What touches your heart and makes you laugh out loud? What were the things you did as a child that were fun? What about today? Again, this becomes important to fuel your energy system and breathe fresh air into your life and lungs.

3. **What are your challenges?** Some of our greatest challenges can also bring clarity and our greatest gifts. I would never wish for anyone to go through what I

had to experience. Yet today, not a day goes by that I'm not filled with gratitude for my amazing family and friends, for the people I meet, and for my clients who trust me with their lives. The reason my Divine Design and Destiny has to do with helping YOU find and fulfill yours is because of the contrast I experienced when I saw how off the beaten path I had gone. However, without the extreme circumstances I went through, although I would have preferred my journey to have been easier, I may never have wound up in the place I am today. And because of my challenges, I believe I have greater empathy and compassion for what you may be experiencing AND the tools for you to get on track much faster.

If you do not find a way to discover the "gold" in your darkest moments, to find a place of forgiveness and a way to reposition yourself, you may be missing a very special opportunity. Sometimes I believe our hurdles and challenges are God's way of putting "bumper guards" in our lives, kind of like the bumper guards that are placed in bowling alleys when kids are learning to bowl. It's a gentle (or not so gentle) way to get you back on track, redirecting your journey.

I'm sure you have read, heard, or even experienced the stories of people who have had horrific events take place in their lives, yet they turn it around to assist others. Your pain can sometimes direct you in your purpose. When you can look adversity in the eye, it will look back, educating and guiding you to a better place.

All of these are clues that can capture your attention and redirect you to your truth and purpose. When you are aware of that, you can then contribute your gifts to others in a most special way.

So it becomes important to work on fueling your mind with the thoughts you want and need to be having, to FEEL in a way that best suits you, which then creates the ENERGY system that guides, directs, connects, and makes some pretty special magic in your life.

WORDS OF ENCOURAGEMENT:

Dear God,

I'm realizing that I have so many blind spots within me. I don't really see how special I am. I don't yet realize that you have given me this life of mine for a special reason and purpose. Please allow me to see what you see. Please help me feel the way you hold me in your heart every day. Please continue to love me, guide me, nourish me, and support me. I am forever grateful for the opportunity you give me each and every moment of every day.

Chapter 13

How Do We Get Off Course and Out of Alignment in the First Place?

Wendy L. Darling

-13-

How Do We Get Out of Alignment and Off Course in the First Place?

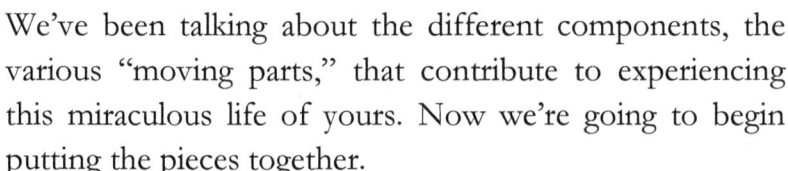

We've been talking about the different components, the various "moving parts," that contribute to experiencing this miraculous life of yours. Now we're going to begin putting the pieces together.

Life has an interesting way of taking you out of alignment and off course, moving you farther away from your authentic path and direction. Given what we now know about how our values, thoughts, and emotions impact the choices and actions we take, it's rather miraculous you've been able to get as far as you have. The relationships you had as a child with your parents and other individuals, your life experiences, and the knowledge regarding how this can impact you—all of these experiences have shaped your personality, the direction you've taken, and the results and quality of life you've lived up to this point.

But if you are reading this book and have gotten this far, you certainly are aware that something is "off," and needs adjusting. Or maybe you've made good progress, but you keep bumping up against the same wall, unable to move to your next level, to take your next step.

So let's begin at the beginning.

When you were a child, you didn't have any boundaries. You and the world were one. On one hand, this is lovely since all you really knew were feelings of love. Whatever experiences you had, you kept putting them into your "love file." (The mind and emotions are always categorizing our experiences.) No matter what the experience, you filed that as love.

So let's say your mother was stressed during pregnancy. That got filed away as love. Or after your birth, she was worried and anxious about being your mom. That got filed away. Or maybe something happened to her or someone was not treating her well. You picked up those feelings and filed them away.

As your brain continued to develop, other experiences were also filed in the love file. And that's how you began defining love!

So let's use the example that your mom wanted you to be "perfect." She watched you closely, your every move. However, as you grew up, she would constantly guide you and correct you. She actually never praised you or even told you she loved you. You learned that "love" meant being criticized. You lacked validation and acknowledgement. You learned that you needed to look outside yourself for love, for answers, for validation.

And that's how you defined love.

So how would something like that play out in your life?

You would grow up NOT knowing what you were good at. You would have issues regarding doubt, insecurities, and your own worthiness. You would have a hard time knowing what to do. It would impact your ability to make good decisions. It would impact your career choices. It would impact the people you would choose as friends, or those you would become involved with intimately.

In some ways, it created a feeling of "being lost" in life. This is one of the most common scenarios I've observed in the people I've served. Somehow, life experiences have taken them to a place of "How did I get here? Is this all there is?" or "I never imagined my life would turn out like this."

Many of these people had successful careers; however, they felt unsatisfied, unfulfilled. Many of these people were challenged in their intimate relationships, wondering why they could not experience lasting love, or why they kept attracting the same kind of person.

These are all symptoms of your misalignment.

SYMPTOMS OF MISALIGNMENT

Instead of beating yourself up, wondering how some of this occurred for you, let's look at these symptoms now as a blessing. You are simply seeing where, at some point, you created a story for what you believed love was to look like and what your best life was to be, but your experiences were not matching what you thought it really should look like.

You knew what you wanted to experience, but you were not experiencing it. You knew you wanted more out of your relationship, but you were not getting it. You knew you wanted more from your career, but you were not experiencing that. These are simply SYMPTOMS of misalignment.

So, take a closer look. This is now a GIFT that is going to show you how to bring yourself back into your truth and natural alignment.

EXERCISE: Write out all the "symptoms" you are currently experiencing in your life. Look at all the categories you listed in your Divine Destiny, "Magic Wand" chapter. The gap is pointing to your symptoms. For example, how is your health? Are you healthy and energetic? Are you fit and at a healthy weight? Do you nourish yourself daily with food, water, and movement? Do you take time each day for prayer and/or meditation or some form of relaxation, stillness, silence? Do the same for the other categories.

Now, write the story that you perceive you created around this. For example, if you are overweight, write the story of "what a person who is overweight thinks about herself." If your desk is a mess, what does that represent to you? The examples below were created to possibly help jump-start your mind and guide you.

Your health: *I don't take care of myself. I work all day. I sit and watch TV. I have no energy or interest in working out. I don't feel like cooking, just picking up and cooking a little something on the spot. I know this isn't good for me, but I keep doing it. I know I need to do more. I'm getting older. I also want to attract a really high-quality man into my life, and if I keep this up, that's not going to happen.*

Conclusions of my misalignment symptoms: *It's not worth trying. I have tried and tried, and nothing ever seems to work out. Life has shown me that I cannot have the body I want, the relationship I want. My desires are not important. I am not worthy of having my desires fulfilled.*

Story:
_____
_____
_____
_____

Conclusions of my misalignment symptoms:

Your home: *I can hardly believe the mess my bedroom and office are. I have piles of clothes; my closets are overflowing. The same goes for my office. I just can't keep up with all the paperwork.*

Conclusions of my misalignment symptoms: *I am having such a hard time focusing on my life. I'm feeling so overwhelmed, worried about all I need to take care of. It's hard to shut off my mind. And every time I look at my office, it gets worse. It makes me stressed to look at my bedroom. Why can't I just relax?*

Story:

Conclusions of my misalignment symptoms:

_____
_____
_____
_____
_____
_____

Your intimate relationship: *What's wrong with me? Why have I not found Mr./Ms. Right for me? I see other people so happy, but somehow I'm beginning to feel I have missed the boat. I don't want to feel needy or desperate, but I'm really irritated that I have not had a relationship in a really long time.*

Conclusions of my misalignment symptoms: *I have chosen so many men/women that have not been right for me. I trust too easily, and I love too fast. Then I find out I gave my heart to the wrong person. After being treated so poorly as a child, having to cope with all the criticism and abuse, it's hard for me to trust and open my heart. Then I go to the opposite extreme, and I open it too fast. I think it's time to learn how to trust myself and to know I deserve love in my life.*

Story:

_____
_____
_____
_____
_____

Conclusions of my misalignment symptoms:

_____
_____
_____
_____
_____
_____

Your Family: *My last child is getting ready to leave home, going off to college. I've devoted so much of my time and attention to my children. As much as I want to let go, I also fear letting go. Even worse, what's going to happen with the relationship with my children, once they are grown and on their own?*

Conclusions of my misalignment symptoms: *My family has been a big part of my life, and I truly love both my children. I can see that as proud as I am for what I've provided for them, it's also been convenient for me not to pay attention to more of my own needs. What am I really afraid of?*

Story:

_____
_____
_____
_____
_____
_____
_____

Conclusions of my misalignment symptoms:

_____
_____
_____
_____
_____
_____
_____

Your friends/community: *I feel so lonely. I spend my day at work, then come home to an empty home. I've lived in this community for almost three years, and I still don't really have a circle of friends. I'd like to be dating, but that doesn't seem to be happening either.*

Conclusions of my misalignment symptoms: *WOW! I've been over-giving at the office. I give so much there, I don't have anything else left for me. I've neglected taking care of myself. I've created a relationship with fast food, the computer, and TV. And I've not had fun in the longest of time. How did that happen?*

Story:

_____
_____
_____
_____
_____
_____

Conclusions of my misalignment symptoms:

___
___
___
___
___
___
___
___

Your career/finances: *I love my work, but something seems to be missing. I put in long hours and get a lot done, but I'm no longer feeling very satisfied. In addition, I'm beginning to feel like I'm being taken for granted. I'm earning the same pay, yet I'm given more responsibilities. I'd like to explore doing something else, but I just don't know what that is.*

Conclusions of my misalignment symptoms: *I didn't realize how much I've wanted a change, but I also feared what that may be. I have not even given myself the opportunity to explore. Maybe, before it's too late, I need to reach out, get some support, and plan for the next chapter in my life.*

Story:

___
___
___
___
___

Conclusions of my misalignment symptoms:

_____
_____
_____
_____
_____
_____
_____

Your fun: *Fun? What's that? Who has time for fun? My job takes most of my time and energy. It's been so long, I don't even know what fun looks like. Sure, I go to a movie from time to time, or maybe get together with a friend or two. But I feel I'm missing out on a lot.*

Conclusions of my misalignment symptoms: *Oh, dear. I have really not allowed myself to explore or get creative. I've managed to get myself in a rut. I can see how this may be one of the reasons I don't have as much energy these days. Life has gotten a little too predictable, a little on the boring side. I don't need much, but it's time to try something new. It may be just the jolt I need.*

Story:

_____
_____
_____
_____
_____
_____
_____

Conclusions of my misalignment symptoms:

_____
_____
_____
_____
_____
_____
_____
_____

Are you beginning to see more of the "stories" you are telling yourself and how you are creating your misalignment? Are you also beginning to see how this may be holding you back from experiencing more joy and happiness in your life? Are you beginning to see how you have settled into a place that is familiar, maybe a bit too comfortable, but it's also robbing you of living a richer and more spectacular life?

In the next chapter, we'll begin bringing you back into alignment.

WORDS OF ENCOURAGEMENT:

Dear God,

I thank you for this wonderful opportunity, this miraculous life you have given me. I now see how I keep myself from all the good you are constantly sending my way. Please take this burden, this misalignment away. Help free me so that I can embrace and enjoy my miraculous life. Help me know my truth. Continue to love, support, and guide me on this miraculous journey, my miraculous life that continues to unfold.

Wendy L. Darling

Chapter 14
Bringing Harmony into Your Heart and Mind

Wendy L. Darling

-14-

Bringing Harmony into Your Heart and Mind

―――――〜―――――

If you are feeling love, that is the place where all possibilities for your life exist. It's the ultimate state where you want to live.

We've been focusing a lot on your targets, the direction you want to head, and the experiences you want to have. We've also been focusing on what isn't working, what's out of alignment, and the distance between where you are and where you want to be. Now we are going to begin the journey of bringing you back into alignment, creating harmony in your heart, your mind, and your life.

We've learned a lot about change in the last fifty years. We've come a long way from the early days of psychology. People like Freud and Jung were the trailblazers of their time. The very thought that life's experiences directly impacted one's life's choices and circumstances was revolutionary.

We've come a long way since then.

Although theories of psychology continued to evolve over the years, other methodologies began emerging. Instead of looking just at someone's past and childhood experiences, more attention was beginning to focus on how the mind works and how it was impacting choices and outcomes of a person's life.

The birth of "new thought" theories and practices began reaching far and wide. Scientists began exploring in greater depth the power of the brain and how the mind works. Technology became more advanced and now enables us to literally track, see, and read brain waves and other activity.

As new evidence emerged, more and more attention began focusing on working with the mind. Creating new thoughts became the next big thing—change your thoughts, change your life.

And there is tremendous validity to that.

One of the first waves of this form of thought-related change work included affirmations. If you said a certain "statement" enough times, it was believed that you would change your outcomes. Unfortunately, for most, it did not. We now know it takes more than creating a new or improved thought to take hold because the older thoughts have greater influence and override your new ones. And these older thoughts are typically not conscious ones. They are living and working under the radar within your subconscious mind, so you are not aware that they are actually alive and well, running wild through the highway of your thoughts, habits, and actions.

We have learned that the subconscious mind, where your attitudes and beliefs are stored, has created very powerful neural pathways that drive the way your mind works. Unfortunately, because they are subconscious, this means that you are unaware that they are actually alive and well. You are unaware of these thoughts.

Remember, you have about 60,000 to 70,000 thoughts a day, and the majority of them come from the subconscious mind. So, your mind is thinking away, commanding away, and you are not aware this is going on.

That's why you tend to keep feeling the same way you do, keep taking similar steps, and even getting in your own way of taking the steps you would prefer to be taking. It's also why, despite your best efforts, you can end up at a very similar place, be with a similar kind of person, and have your bank account get to the same place, as well.

Another key point is that many theories and methodologies had you looking at your past in order to try and find what was out of balance, where the hurts and heartaches originated. I used to do this for myself, and my clients.

Then, one day, I found myself asking the question: *If we know the mind is the motor, directing our emotions and actions and influencing our energy systems…WHAT IF WE'VE BEEN LOOKING IN THE WRONG DIRECTION?*

Let me explain a little more what I was exploring.

I knew that the mind is a very powerful instrument. I knew that it is one of the major driving forces creating results. They may be the results you want, but they also could be the ones that you don't.

But I realized I was always looking for what wasn't working, what was out of alignment. It created a scenario where I believed that something was wrong, something needed to be fixed and adjusted. And THIS was creating a barrier in itself.

So I set out to do an experiment.

I decided to take my Healing Harmonics™ System and put it to work in a different way. I made a new recording using my sound healing. I picked a couple of my healing cards, and I created some statements that I wanted my mind to be thinking that would support my efforts. In my case, I had gained some weight, so I used this as an experiment to see what kind of change could occur, and to see if it would be AS effective, or possibly even more effective.

I used my process first thing in the morning and in the evening right before going to sleep.

My results were profound. I started feeling better about my body. I began noticing I was gravitating to foods that I knew supported my body. Even when I had a treat, I enjoyed every bite and didn't have the negative or critical "chatter" regarding my choice. And best of all? There was no more criticism of my body. I found myself waking up in the morning WANTING to get some movement and/or exercise—I was doing this organically, regularly, with the greatest of ease. Within a short period of time (about three months), I had released a little over twenty pounds.

What I loved about my experiment—especially choosing weight loss as the result I wanted—was I had physical evidence that my theory worked. This is how Healing Harmonics™ was officially birthed!

I was overjoyed, and I began incorporating this way of creating an easier way to change with my clients. It has worked with each and every person since that time!

In fact, my very first client was a woman who wanted to release weight. She had tried every diet under the sun with little to no success. As we began, and immediately following her first session with me, her weight began falling off her body. She released twenty pounds in her first month. In her second month, she released another twenty pounds. Eventually, she released over sixty pounds, and she was able to get off nine of her ten medications. She also loved how her relationship with her husband renewed, as they experienced more intimacy and a deeper connection. Time with her children became sweeter. Even their home got more organized. And, within our time together, she found a better job that increased her salary.

This is just one example of hundreds.

Now, I want to add one more component.

It's not just the mind that's important to focus on.

The emotions are really the ultimate state you want to experience. Your thoughts point you in the direction of how you want to be FEELING. If you are feeling happy, you can rest assured there are happy thoughts associated with that. If you are feeling worried, you can rest assured that there are thoughts feeding into your doubt and concern.

If you are feeling love, that is the place where all possibilities for your life exist. It's the ultimate state where you want to live.

So it is critical that you form a healthy partnership between your heart and mind. The partnership between these two creates the sweet spot for living your miraculous life, for you to experience your Divine Destiny, for you to simply live a happy, healthy, and prosperous life.

I am SO grateful that I am one of the people providing an easier, faster, simpler, and most effective way for you to shift into your divine plan and path for your life, to finally experience all the riches and wonders life has to offer.

HAPPY THOUGHT + HAPPY HEART = HAPPY LIFE

EXERCISE: Think about a person or situation where you can easily experience a feeling of love. (For me, I think about my sweet man, my son, or I simply imagine looking out at the ocean.) Write down as many thoughts as you can as you think about this (e.g., I cannot believe how blessed I am to have him in my life. I have been given the most miraculous gift. I am in awe of the beauty of the ocean. I feel blessed to be standing here right now. I am grateful for this experience. What a miraculous world we live in.). Do this exercise in the morning as you begin your day, especially if you may not find it easy to experience love. Do the same in the evening before going to bed. Of course, if you take a few "love breaks" during your day, you'll find your day will be easier, smoother, and even more productive. The purpose of this exercise is to have you presence the feeling of love.

WORDS OF ENCOURAGEMENT:

Dear God,

I thank you, once again, for the blessings in my life. I thank you for this miraculous life you have given me, for my generous and extraordinary heart. Please continue to guide me, nourish me, and support me to find the courage to take the steps I need to take to continue this journey. Help me live in my heart, allowing it to guide me each and every step of the way. Help me remember that all we really need is love. Help me be one of the beacons that shines love from me to the rest of the world.

Chapter 15

Mischief Makers

Wendy L. Darling

-15-

Mischief Makers

In life, you are either making magic, or making mischief

WOW! As I'm attempting to write this chapter, I cannot even believe all the mischief-makers that have crept up. I've fixed my lunch and cleaned my dishes; my countertops are sparkling; I've checked e-mail at least twice, been on Facebook, and called my mom and sisters. Are you getting an idea of how mischief-makers can show up in your life? At least I can now put much of that to good use as I continue to write. You see, I have a (self-imposed) deadline to finish this chapter before I leave for a meeting in LA, and because I like keeping on a timeline, meeting my deadlines (and even staying ahead of them) is important to me. So I'm going to tame my urges, sit my body down, and WRITE. (I'll let you know how it goes by the end of the chapter.)

In these next two chapters we're going to take a look at what happens when you set your sights on a goal, begin taking steps ... and then suddenly realize you simply are not making the progress you want to be making.

Remember those internal communications we addressed earlier, the ones you are having with yourself all the time? You can be pretty sure that they have something to do with your journey and progress.

In this first chapter we're going to take a closer look at your personality, at who you tend to be. In the next chapter, we'll look more closely at the experiences you tend to create.

In my world, you are either Making Magic or Making Mischief.

Making Magic involves listening to your intuition, following divine inspiration, and taking the steps that serve and support who you are and what best works for you, and that enrich your life so that you can continue down the path of your Divine Destiny.

Making Mischief, on the other hand, is what you do that gets you off track, off your path. It's what causes you to deflect all those good intentions, your guidance, your Divine Destiny. And it's important to be aware of what you are doing so that you can shift that and experience more of the life and results you desire.

So it basically boils down to this: Are you deflecting, or are you opening yourself to receive, and to allow yourself to experience your life, the Divine Destiny way?

So let's look at some common Mischief-Makers:

1. **The mischief of shiny objects.** Are you someone that gets intrigued, even seduced by, a new idea, yet at the same time, you find it difficult to complete? Then you find yourself off and running to something new? It's important to look at what's really going on. What's making you jump from one thing to another? Are you not valuing yourself, your time? What might you be avoiding by NOT completing a task?

2. **The mischief of details.** Are you the kind of person that gets lost in details, making certain that you research all the facts, read, and reread? Are you concerned that you will miss something? What is driving this? When is enough, enough?

3. **The mischief of perfectionism.** This is a cousin to the mischief of details. This is how you make certain all your *t*'s are crossed and all your *i*'s are dotted. I can remember the first training program I wrote—it took months. I was so concerned that my program would not have enough information and exercises, and I never felt like it was "done." If this sounds familiar to you, what are you afraid of?

Why are you setting your expectation bar so high that you'll never allow yourself to be satisfied?

4. **The mischief of ADD (Attention Deficit).** This is another relative of The Mischief of Shiny Objects. These are all the little distractions you allow to get in the way of a project or task. Just as I mentioned above, I had resistance to sitting down and writing. Somehow I wasn't feeling like this chapter would flow, so I avoided even starting to write. However, as soon as I started … well, I'm still writing. So you need to first catch yourself and ask yourself what is making you uncomfortable. What is it about this task, step, or project that you may not want to face? What are you telling yourself? Take an honest look. It may be feelings of inadequacy, or maybe you think it's going to take too much time and energy, etc. I used to feel this way when I needed to do my income taxes. Although I still have a little resistance around doing them, it's minor in comparison.

5. **The mischief of social media.** I just have to list this. I don't know about you, but I could make a career out of reading e-mails and looking at Facebook posts and other information the Internet places at our fingertips. For me, it takes discipline and structure. In fact, I refuse to spend time looking at e-mail the very first thing in the

morning. I typically check e-mail only once in the morning, and then again in the evening. Occasionally I'll check midday. This is an area that I continue to strengthen, each time with determination. I've gotten really good at deleting A LOT of e-mails. (I used to be so curious about what others were sending out.) I have also gotten better at deleting myself from other people's lists. I recently changed e-mail addresses and am slowly getting off even more lists. Even though I have a message telling them not to use my previous e-mail address they have not taken the time to take me off their lists. Take a really close look at how much time you dedicate to e-mail and social media. I was recently chastised a bit for not interacting very often with a private Facebook group. I don't know about you, but I have things I need to be doing, and I have to get them done.

6. **The mischief of taking care of the small stuff.** Sometimes when there is a bigger task to take on, there is a tendency to do the small stuff, thinking you are making progress. This is simply another avoidance tactic, but you are at least accomplishing something, so it feels a little better. In this case, I suggest you take your larger task and break it down into small, manageable steps. Then schedule the time to do that step with a beginning time and an ending time. Sometimes, when there is a big

project or task, you keep trying to get a large block of time to work on it, but that may not be realistic. Instead, chunk down the times and use that time exclusively for that one task. Not only will you feel a sense of accomplishment, but you are also building trust with yourself. You are training your mind that you will do what you say you are going to do, in the time you've allotted to do it. You will be amazed how much you get done in a short amount of time. I laugh at myself when I see how I'm avoiding a task, but then it takes me no time at all to accomplish it. Make sure you schedule the most important tasks/projects first, then fill in the rest of your calendar with the items of lesser importance.

7. **The mischief of not doing what you say you are going to do.** I see this ALL the time (and, yes, this has happened to me more than I care to confess, saying you will do something and you don't). This may be with a work-related task, a friend, or a family member. However, it's more likely a commitment that you have made to yourself. We neglect our own word and commitments way too easily. Over time, it should be no surprise that you no longer trust yourself to follow through with your words, your promises now. A most common example is when someone decides to drop a few—or more than a few—

pounds. You decide to eat a certain way and/or get more exercise. Maybe you decide you want to take time in the morning for meditation and prayer. The way you care for yourself represents either Making Magic or Making Mischief, but this habit CAN be changed. And for your personal good, for you to experience more health, happiness, and wealth in your life, it's time to take those small steps, rebuilding trust in yourself and your word, building the muscle of doing what you say you are going to do.

8. **The mischief of putting someone else's needs before yours.** Don't get me wrong. I know that we all have certain responsibilities, and for some of you, you have many people depending on you. But remember to put your oxygen mask on first. Interestingly enough, I find those that give so much of themselves and their time are actually starved and in need of receiving more attention and support. What can you do to nourish yourself first, but then be available for the people and responsibilities in your life?

9. **The mischief of blind spots.** Uh, oh. This is the trickiest of them all because you are not even really aware of what you may be doing. So what's a person to do? Simply take a look at what you have wanted to accomplish and see if you are

accomplishing it. Is there a way to take a closer look at the time spent? Maybe you can ask a spouse, family member, or friend if they have noticed anything. Maybe it's time to hire a coach or mentor. I remember not knowing why so much time would pass in my day, and I would hardly accomplish a thing. This was many years ago, and it's a very extreme example, but through my questioning, I discovered I had a brain injury that had never been diagnosed. Had I not inquired, I possibly would not be writing this book right now. This taught me to ask others what their experience was of me, as well as any other ideas and feedback they might have.

10. **The mischief of the glass ceiling.** This is an important one to watch out for that typically has to do with feelings of self-worth. It plays out in a variety of ways. You may hit the glass ceiling of your income. You get to a certain place with the money you make, but find you always spend it all. You may have a budget but never seem to be able to stick with it. Finances are one of the most common glass-ceiling symptoms. Weight is another one. You start a health plan, but within a short period of time, you stop working out, or you begin overeating. Or you reach a certain weight and are unable to get past that number on the scale; even more typical, you begin gaining your weight back.

You have inadvertently created a barrier that doesn't allow you to go further to experience your deepest desires. Although this is typical in all the mischief-makers, this one becomes very apparent since it typically hits the areas of your deepest desires. This is where Healing Harmonics™ provides the biggest opportunity for silencing those mischief-makers and shattering the glass ceiling, making room for the real you to emerge.

11. **The mischief of worry and doubt.** Lions and tigers and bears, oh my! This is one of the most common mischief-makers of all. When you are working on a new task or a large project, or embarking on a new goal, walking in new territory, the mind simply has a field day. When you find yourself in a place where you don't know what to do, your mind gets overly active, searching for solutions. It can be a very unsettling time. Not trusting that you will find what you need to find and that you will do what you need to do creates a lot of worry. Worry is simply creating doubt around a future that has not even happened. If you can remember that, KNOW that you do not have to have all the answers right now, and that if you can take just that ONE step, you will know your next step right when you need to know what that might be. It's time to TRUST in yourself and life. I

know it's not always easy, but if you strengthen your TRUST muscle, it will carry you far.

There are obviously many more Mischief-Makers that can be listed, but hopefully this can at least open your eyes a little more and help you notice when you may be Making Magic … and when you are Making Mischief. Typically these are just the patterns and habits that have created interference, holding you back from the life you were born to live.

I encourage you not to give up. Continue taking your steps because your miraculous life, your Divine Destiny is lighting up the path of perfection. It doesn't mean it's going to be "perfect." It just means that your path is perfect for you.

EXERCISE: Think about goals, tasks, and projects you've had in the past. How smoothly were you able to accomplish them? What are some of your mischief-makers? What takes you away from getting the results you want? Let's look at your original categories and see where you tend to Make Magic and where you tend to Make Mischief. Even if there are a couple areas where mischief lives more frequently, take some time to look at the small steps you can begin to take to make a little more magic in your life.

SPIRITUAL MISCHIEF
SPIRITUAL MAGIC

HOME MISCHIEF
HOME MAGIC

HEALTH MISCHIEF
HEALTH MAGIC

LOVE MISCHIEF
LOVE MAGIC

FAMILY MISCHIEF
FAMILY MAGIC

FRIENDS/COMMUNITY MISCHIEF
FRIENDS/COMMUNITY MAGIC

CAREER/FINANCE MISCHIEF
CAREER/FINANCE MAGIC

FUN MISCHIEF
FUN MAGIC

The area that I want to make more magic is:

_____
_____
_____
_____

The steps I will take now are:

_____

_____

_____

_____

WORDS OF ENCOURAGEMENT:

Dear God,

I thank you for supporting me in my journey. I appreciate the opportunity to see how I keep you and all the good you are trying to send my way at an arm's length. Help me relax more into my life. Help me find more trust in you and myself. And help me appreciate and celebrate the magic that this miraculous life you have given me offers.

Wendy L. Darling

Chapter 16

Speed Bumps, Detours and Roadblocks

Wendy L. Darling

-16-

Speed Bumps, Detours and Road Blocks

Ah, the mysteries of life. It certainly has a way of encouraging us, moving us forward, slowing us down, even having us stop to a halt. Yet, instead of looking at these "slower" moments with sadness, frustration, or anger, I want you to explore the richness these moments can provide.

I truly believe that you are being guided, in each and every moment, to fulfill your Divine Destiny. I believe we have a most spectacular opportunity to learn, to grow, and to BE the divine person you were created to be, to live the extraordinary, miraculous life that was designed specifically for you. And the only thing getting in the way of experiencing all the riches life has to offer … is you.

SPEED BUMPS: Speed bumps slow you down, just a bit. In fact, I think I'm having one of those moments right now. I want to finish this chapter within the next hour. Yet, I've found myself playing with my dog, going to get some water, and now I just came back with a small square of dark chocolate. (Who doesn't want to enjoy a little indulgence while working on a Saturday afternoon?)

See what I mean?

That's a speed bump. It's slowing me down.

On the other hand though, it also gave me a break, which I probably needed. So a speed bump isn't a bad thing. It's just a speed bump. You get to decide if slowing down a bit is a good thing, or if it's taking you away from what you are doing.

In this case, I vote that I needed a break. And right now, I'm writing away; the words are flowing out of my fingers with ease.

DETOURS: A detour is something that happens in your life and takes you off course, possibly just temporarily, but eventually returns you to your best path. Maybe you were working on a project, but your child needed your attention (homework? driving them to a game?). Or maybe you've been spending a little too much time on that project, and your family is calling you to spend time with THEM. That's pretty important.

Then, of course, there could be times when you need to get the next phase of your project done, but you can hear your family having a great time and you want to join in.

In this case, I always recommend creating a way to structure your time—literally scheduling project/work time, family time, YOU time, etc. Set start times and end times. Otherwise you can get caught in the loop of a detour and not be satisfied, much less, not accomplish what you want and need to be doing.

You'll see that it's amazing what you can accomplish when you set parameters to your schedule.

I can remember when my son was very young, I had a fairly demanding job. It was one of those jobs for which my "to-do" list just kept growing. But I learned how to STOP, leave it alone, and focus on my family. What I found most interesting after doing this was that I became even more focused and productive. Since my son needed attention first thing in the morning, I would get a workout at noon, having packed a lunch so that I could eat it as soon as I got back. (This was at a time when there was a gym in the building where I worked, which made it really easy.) Other times, I would just go out for walks.

By the way, taking those breaks, catching your breath, and going for a short walk can make a HUGE difference in your productivity.

ROADBLOCKS: These are the times that you simply feel stopped. You've bumped up against a wall, and you are not sure what you need to do.

This is a great time to use what I call the Red Light, Yellow Light, Green Light Decision-Making process.

Red light — This is just as it sounds. You are stopped. But the gift of this experience is to examine what is going on that has stopped you. Have you been pushing yourself, and are you now headed in the wrong direction? Is this a warning sign that trouble lies ahead and you need to pay attention? It can also mean that it is time to take a brief time-out, catch your breath, regroup, and begin again. Only you know. But when you hit that wall, you need to stop. Trying to bump up against it, without reflection, will not work on your behalf. Pay attention. Follow your hunch. What might this roadblock be attempting to tell you?

Green light — This is also clear and easy to determine. There is no doubt, just inspiration to take your next step. You may still feel a bit of discomfort, even a tinge (or more) of fear, but you KNOW in every fiber of your being that you are to move forward. This is the place where magic, miracles, and inspiration live. Learn to trust it, follow it … and move forward with confidence.

Yellow Light — These are the moments when you find yourself going back and forth. One second you think "yes," while the next is a "no." So you live in that uncomfortable place of "maybe" land. At the same time, however, a yellow light is also a gift. It's a time of reflection. It's when you need to take a step back and see what may be contributing to your uncertainty. And, because of this uncertainty, a yellow light always turns into a red light since you must pause and reassess before taking any further action. There is wisdom in this pause. It can mean the timing is not right. It can mean you need more information or a slightly different action. It can also mean that one of your mischief makers has taken over, preventing you from moving forward. One way to determine this: you keep taking a certain number of steps, but you get stopped at a certain point and can no longer move forward. If this has happened more than once, you can be certain your mind is creating the interference.

Remember, life is kind of like a Rubik's cube. There are lots of moving parts, but as you make minor adjustments, you can actually experience significant results. A ship only has to alter its course less than one degree to shift its direction and destination significantly. Your life is designed in a similar manner.

So I want you to appreciate these times when you hit a speed bump, a detour, or a roadblock. You are ALWAYS being guided to experience your highest good, your Divine Destiny, and these moments are gifts from the heavens, making sure that you stay present to all that is being provided for you in your wonderful, magical, and miraculous life!

EXERCISE: To help you become aware of the gifts of speed bumps, detours, and roadblocks, I want you to reflect back on some of your past experiences. I want you to remember a time when each of these have taken place, and I want you to now see the gift each of these experiences has provided. Having done this, I want you to REMEMBER that these moments truly are gifts. And hopefully, from this point forward, you will allow yourself to be more aware, pay more attention, and allow the magic of your miraculous life to unfold with great ease and significantly more joy.

SPEED BUMP:

_____
_____
_____
_____

The gold of this experience is:

_____
_____
_____
_____

DETOUR:

_____
_____
_____
_____

The gold of this experience is:

_____
_____
_____
_____

ROADBLOCK:

_____
_____
_____
_____

The gold of this experience is:

_____
_____
_____
_____

Wendy L. Darling

WORDS OF ENCOURAGEMENT:

Dear God,

Please continue to guide me on my journey of living this miraculous life you have so graciously provided for me. Allow me to see, hear, and feel your wisdom, your love, your guidance. Help me stay awake and aware of these magical moments. Help me to appreciate all my moments, even those I question. Allow me to discover the magic of life, trusting how it unfolds, appreciating the magnificence of each and every moment, and living in gratitude for all that you provide. I am forever grateful for these golden opportunities you constantly provide.

Chapter 17

Healing Harmonics™ and Your Signature Soul Song™

Wendy L. Darling

-17-

Healing Harmonics™ and Your Signature Soul Song™

I am now going to share the system many people have used to help them finally shift into the life they were born to live. It's what I've named Healing Harmonics™. I wish I could tell you exactly why I chose this name. In fact, it may have chosen me. But the healing that comes through this process, bringing harmony into your body and your life, is beyond awesome. There is not a day that goes by that I do not feel a sense of gratitude.

As I shared in the beginning of this book, I was not always a healer. I was a management and organizational development consultant. Blending both of these worlds, though, has provided me with the opportunity to assist people to change in a much easier and faster way, as my consulting skills assist my clients to position themselves for success. It's an approach like no other.

So let me explain, in greater detail, the Healing Harmonics™ system.

First of all, I am able to see and feel energy, and I am guided, very intuitively, as to what to do and how to do it.

Part of my process involves me "singing." I basically open myself up to receive the love God is sending to you, to move stuck energy, remove it, and then infuse you with a new, loving energy. This loving, healing energy comes from the heavens. It's pure love. When I do this, I have seen people change literally right before my very eyes.

But before I begin this portion of the process, I have a comprehensive diagnostic system I use that identifies the ROOT CAUSE of what is interfering and holding you back. It's the source of your misalignment. It's what is causing you to struggle or simply not experience the results you desire.

Then I do my healing work through my singing. I also have Vibrational Healing Cards. These designs came through me during meditations.

In many ways, creating these Healing Cards was like a spiritual paint-by-numbers experience. I would start with a sheet of paper, initially drawing these in magic marker. I later "advanced" to creating these designs in glitter glue.

And what is even more amazing is, when copied, they retain their power. They still are just as effective as the originals.

I then receive certain colors that you are to work with. Again, this supports you in both the releasing process and in strengthening you and your life. It varies from person to person and changes over the course of our time working together.

Then, either I create a customized Healing Harmonics™ package. I 'receive' statements—what many would consider affirmations—that are used with the process to begin retraining the mind. The beauty of this is that not only are you creating and strengthening your neural pathways, the highways of your thoughts, but as you use the statements with the sound healing and cards, it literally will wash away anything that is NOT in alignment. When you say your statement out loud, anything that is NOT in alignment with this statement will rise to the conscious surface, almost in protest. The process, however, melts it all away, saying "bye-bye" to the very thoughts and feelings that have been creating mischief in your life.

For more information on how you can receive you very own, customized Healing Harmonics™ – Signature Soul Song package:

http://wendydarling.com/signature-soul-song/

WORDS OF ENCOURAGEMENT:

Dear God,

Allow your words, your voice, and your sounds of love to surround me and move through me. Let your love gently melt away the layers that have kept the real me from emerging. I am grateful for the opportunity to finally be free, to finally be able to be me!

Chapter 18
Putting Your Miracle of Life Method into Practice

Wendy L. Darling

-18-

Putting Your *Miracle of Life* Method into Practice

───≈───

It's now time to bring all the pieces together. In this chapter I'm going to walk you through your daily practices that will allow you to come into alignment and harmony with your Divine Design and Destiny. Remember, keep these practices simple. The intention is to help you RELAX so that you can live in your body, listen to and follow the guidance of your heart, and have the strength and determination to be in action.

Let's look at the steps that best support your wonderful journey:

1. **Begin your day in silence**. The sooner you do this upon awakening, the easier it will be. Since you

are rested, your mind is more relaxed, more pliable. It's easier to go into a meditation, continuing to soothe your mind.

2. **Take time in your morning to journal.** A wonderful way to clear your mind and position yourself for the day ahead is to write. I recommend you begin your day in gratitude. Write at last five things for which you are grateful. Gratitude opens your heart for the blessings that already exist. I also suggest you recognize and write gratitude for the blessings you are about to receive. There is magic with living in certainty. Give thanks to God for the new client, the new job, for a peaceful resolution to a challenge. FEEL how good it feels to experience this. Whatever it is, express gratitude. When you accept what will be as your truth, that it's a "done deal," you align with the frequency of this, and it flows to you with greater ease and speed. Living in a state of "as if," meaning living in the state of it already is a done deal, creates the "done deal"!

3. **Ask God to share whatever s/he wishes to share with you.** If you have a question, ask the question. If you need clarity or an idea, ask. If you want words of encouragement or a message of guidance, ask for that. Spend time in silence, and use the Healing Harmonics™ System.

4. **Use the Healing Harmonics™ System** (using sounds, vibrational healing cards, color and statements). Part of the process is choosing your color for the day. What might yours be? Remember, I'm interested in you tuning into your natural frequency. When you are in alignment, meaning your thoughts and emotions are SUPPORTING you, that's when miracles show up and you are in the natural flow of your life.

5. **Focus on your target/your results.** Spend time focusing on your ultimate results. Keep your mind and EMOTIONS on the experience you are creating. Also focus on the results and experiences you want to have by the end of your day. How do you want to FEEL? Allow yourself to FEEL what it will feel like to have this day complete. How does it feel to have experienced and accomplished all that you intend to accomplish?

6. **Schedule your day.** If you are not clear on what you want and need to accomplish in your day, make your list now. Be specific with your tasks. Prioritize your tasks. Follow the 80/20 rule: spend 80 percent of your time with the 20 percent that produces your greatest results. (Too often, people will focus on trivial tasks, thinking they are accomplishing something—e.g., e-mails, Facebook, and other social media.) Structure your time

frames. Be sure to have a beginning and an ending time—and honor your schedule. You will be amazed by how much you accomplish when you focus and structure your time this way.

7. **Take action.** Yep. Begin taking those steps! I don't think I need to say anything else.

8. **Acknowledge and celebrate your progress.** With each task you complete, take a moment and check it off your list and give yourself a "high five." When you have many tasks to do, it's easy to just feel like there is one less task, and you jump right into the next. Acknowledging your progress actually makes a difference in your energy system. It keeps you feeling good about what you are doing. Be sure to acknowledge each and every step. Don't wait until you finish a whole project or task. Promise?

9. **Assess and reassess.** This is important as well. It's important to see if you are taking the steps that are closing your gap. You need to determine if you are on track or need to adjust a bit. A plan is just that. All plans need to be adjusted once executed. It's part of the refining process.

10. **Rinse and repeat.** This is all that's necessary. You now know the process. Remember to keep your

eye on the target; assess and evaluate regularly, and course correct as needed. Consistency and a willingness to keep moving forward are key to your success, to your ability to enjoy the journey of your miraculous life!

WORDS OF ENCOURAGEMENT:

Dear God,

I am tremendously grateful for how I am beginning to really see who I am. I am in awe of the life you have given me, the path that has been laid out for me, and I now realize the partnership we have, with you guiding me every step of the way. I commit to taking time each day to hear you, feel you, and listen to you. Continue to instill the courage and determination for me not only to take steps in this miraculous journey, but to also empower me to forever express my gratitude for the life you allow me to live each and every day. I am forever grateful.

Chapter 19

Finding H.O.M.E.

Wendy L. Darling

-19-
Finding H.O.M.E.

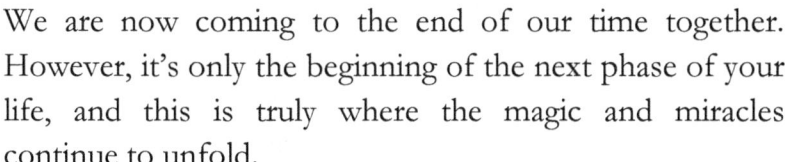

We are now coming to the end of our time together. However, it's only the beginning of the next phase of your life, and this is truly where the magic and miracles continue to unfold.

I know my life has had amazing twists and turns as I learned how to cultivate all that I've shared with you, and it continues to amaze me, delight me, and sometimes challenge me. But the one place that does not seem to go away is my ultimate faith and trust that I am living the life I was designed to live. I am in gratitude for the miraculous opportunity and life I get to honor and celebrate each and every day.

What really matters is that you feel "at home" in your skin and your life, which is why I created an acronym for H.O.M.E. It stands for:

    H – Heaven

    O – On

    E – Earth

    M – With Me in the Middle

That's what I believe life is all about—Heaven on Earth … With Me/You in the Middle. I believe we have the opportunity to experience an incredible life if we remove anything interfering and holding ourselves back, and if we relax into the magnificence that literally surrounds each and every one of us, each and every day.

The challenges that you have possibly faced are simply showing you the gap. Now you have tools that can aid you in closing it. Remember, all of this is being designed in a way to bring you H.O.M.E. Home is where the heart is. Home is where you reside. Being "home" in your body and your life is simply the best.

I can now be grateful for each and every one of the moments of my life. Do I wish it could have been easier? Absolutely. Do I wish I would have learned and adjusted sooner? You bet. But how can I resent a single moment (now) when I have so many blessings today in my life? I can't.

If my life would have been shaped differently, I never would have uncovered my healing gift and process. Had I not had the challenges to overcome, I probably would not be so grateful for the smallest of experiences that now bring me some of my greatest moments of joy.

Even on the days when life still throws me a bit of a curve ball, a bit of a challenge, it's so very easy to now "course correct," to determine what needs to be different, and then do it. Or even those times when my heart may hurt from experiencing a disappointment, I can be with my feelings, experience them, which ultimately sets them free. I no longer fear my feelings, especially the ones that don't feel good. But by being open to the vulnerability of being hurt, I also open my heart to experience more love and joy. Fortunately, in my life today, the majority of my life is lived experiencing love, appreciation, gratitude, and a bunch of happiness. One of the easiest things for me to experience in my life today: smiling.

I promise you, if I learned how to do this … it's going to be even easier for you. You don't have to create a road map. I've done that for you. You don't have to go on a treasure hunt, trying to find what's out of alignment. I can help you. And you certainly don't have to take one more step alone! I'm here for you.

I thank you from the bottom of my heart for sharing this time together. There is NOTHING more important than supporting those in my personal and professional life to be who they authentically are, to live an authentic life, and to share your magnificence, in your own unique way, with the rest of the world.

You are a gift. You are special. And you were created to live a wonderful, miraculous life.

Because, it's not just your life that's miraculous ...

WHO YOU ARE IS THE TRUE MIRACLE!

WORDS OF ENCOURAGEMENT:

Dear God,

Thank you for the life you have given me and for the gifts I get to experience each and every day. Help me continue to see the magnificence in my moments. Help me continue to open my heart and share my love with those who are in my life. Continue to guide me to also share my heart, my gifts, and my skills with kindness and humility to those I am able to serve. And may I use my miraculous life in a way that helps make this world a better place.

Wendy L. Darling

About the Author

Wendy L. Darling, Life Transformation Expert

Wendy L. Darling, founder of Thumbprints International, LLC., offers presentations, seminars, and private mentoring/coaching. She is the creator of Healing HarmonicsTM, a transformational system, allowing her clients to achieve their desired results in a faster and easier manner.

Wendy has over 30 years of experience as a life transformation expert, management and organizational development consultant, manager and executive, entrepreneur, radio talk show personality and keynote speaker.

Wendy has a way of presenting simple, yet profound questions, ideas and thoughts in a way that her clients are motivated, but more important, inspired to action. She has a way of guiding people to the core of their desires, wishes and needs, navigating them to discover the best path to reach their target. She blends traditional business ideas with innovative techniques and practical life skills. Also important, she is a visionary, calling for new ideas, new practices, and new methods of operation.

Wendy has designed and delivered more than 50 seminar and presentation topics to well over 200,000 people across the U.S. Some of her signature presentations and programs include:

- *Is Your Bottom Impacting Your Bottom Line?*
- *Winning At Business By Mastering Your Inner Game*
- *I.D. Your Success Trifecta*
- *Making The Connection – Attracting Love Into Your Life*
- and *Loving Yourself Lean (a permanent solution for weight loss)*

In addition, Wendy has provided consulting and keynote presentations to some of the country's leading organizations.

Wendy formerly wrote a Positive Parenting column, is a former contributing columnist for *Metro Family, Dallas Family* and *Today's Dallas Woman, Today's Innovative Woman* and hosted her own radio shows on CBS The Sky Radio, and in Boca Raton, Fla. She has been featured in Forbes and other publications, and as a guest on numerous radio and TV shows.

Wendy holds a Bachelor of Science degree in education, a Master of Education in counseling psychology and personnel services and a Specialist's degree from the University of Missouri, Columbia. Clients have dubbed Wendy as their personal "fairy godmother" for her ability to help them live the life of their dreams.

THE MIRACLE THAT IS YOUR LIFE

Wendy L. Darling

Connect with Wendy

Learn more about Wendy and all her unique tools and programs at:

http://wendydarling.com/

http://lovinglean.com/

Email:

wendy@wendydarling.com

Facebook:

https://www.facebook.com/wendy.darling.8

Linked In:

linkedin.com/in/wendydarling1

Wendy L. Darling

In Gratitude to You

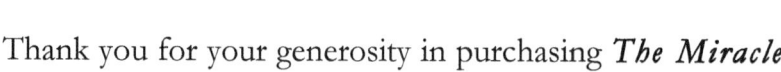

Thank you for your generosity in purchasing *The Miracle That Is Your Life*.

I would be so grateful if you could take a minute or two to share what you loved about this book and provide an honest review on our Amazon sales page.

www.ingramcontent.com/pod-product-compliance
Lightning Source LLC
Chambersburg PA
CBHW071454040426
42444CB00008B/1329